SIMPLY KEYNES

GREAT LIVES

ROGER BACKHOUSE

Simply Charly

Simply Keynes

For permissions or inquiries, contact: permissions@casacarlini.com

ISBN (Paperback): 978-1-943657-88-9

ISBN (eBook): 978-1-943657-87-2

First Edition: 2023

Printed in the United States of America

OTHER GREAT LIVES

Simply Austen

Simply Beckett

Simply Beethoven

Simply Chekhov

Simply Chinggis

Simply Chomsky

Simply Chopin

Simply Darwin

Simply Descartes

Simply Dickens

Simply Dirac

Simply Eliot

Simply Faulkner

Simply Gödel

Simply Hegel

Simply Hitchcock

Simply Joyce

Simply Nabokov

Simply Napoleon

Simply Nietzsche

Simply Proust

Simply Riemann

Simply Sartre

Simply Stravinsky

Simply Tolstoy

Simply Turing

Simply Wittgenstein

PRAISE FOR SIMPLY KEYNES

Keynes stands with Adam Smith and Karl Marx among history's most influential economic thinkers, but, like his illustrious predecessors, is often misunderstood by friend and foe alike. Roger Backhouse's *Simply Keynes* provides an antidote via its engaging and eminently readable account of Keynes' life, ideas, and impact on economic policymaking. From Versailles to Bretton Woods to modern policy debates, Backhouse shows us why Keynes mattered and continues to matter.

— STEVEN G. MEDEMA, RESEARCH PROFESSOR IN THE DEPARTMENT OF ECONOMICS, DUKE UNIVERSITY

Brief, readable, and written from today's perspective, this book makes a persuasive case for the contemporary relevance of Keynes' life and work. Highly recommended, either as an introduction to the subject or, for older readers, a refresher course.

— DAVID ERNEST WILLIAM LAIDLER, PROFESSOR EMERITUS, DEPARTMENT OF ECONOMICS, UNIVERSITY OF WESTERN ONTARIO

John Maynard Keynes and his important ideas shaped economic analysis and economic policy for many decades of the 20th century. The distinguished historian of economics, Roger E. Backhouse, has written a concise book that presents the man and his ideas to non-specialist readers. Eschewing uninformed left-right polemics that have shaped popular discussions of macroeconomics, Backhouse presents the intellectual and historical contexts of Keynesianism's creation, growth, development, and lasting impact. It is a virtuoso performance by a renowned Keynes scholar.

— E. ROY WEINTRAUB, PROFESSOR EMERITUS OF ECONOMICS, DUKE UNIVERSITY

Roger Backhouse combines the skills of a historian with those of an economist, helping us not only to know Keynes, but also to learn about the development of macroeconomics from the demise of its ideas and their vindication in the post-COVID-19 world. Non-specialists and specialists alike can appreciate this concise, but exhaustive, clear, and scholarly account of Keynes and Keynesianism and their relevance. It shows that Keynes is someone whose insights are still relevant and a more interesting thinker than much modern commentary gives him credit for.

— MARIA CRISTINA MARCUZZO, PROFESSOR IN POLITICAL ECONOMY, UNIVERSITY OF ROME

Roger Backhouse's *Simply Keynes* is simply the best brief account of Keynes' thought and influence. Keynes was a man of parts, and Backhouse draws those parts together to form a lucid and compelling portrait of the most influential economist of the 20th century.

— KEVIN HOOVER, PROFESSOR OF ECONOMICS AND PHILOSOPHY, DUKE UNIVERSITY

John Maynard Keynes is the first economist portrayed in Simply Charly's "Great Lives" series, as part of a distinguished set of the world's most influential people (e.g., Freud, Einstein, Darwin, Beethoven, Sartre, Napoleon, Proust), who left an extended legacy in several domains. Roger Backhouse's sparkling account goes beyond biographical information, providing an enlightening history of the evolution of macroeconomic theory and policy from about 100 years ago until nowadays, as seen from the perspective of Keynes' seminal contributions. Written in pleasant and accessible language, the book makes a complex history look simple, with its masterful blend of Keynes' ideas, their origins, impact, and (sometimes critical) reception.

— MAURO BOIANOVSKY, PROFESSOR OF ECONOMICS, UNIVERSITY OF BRASÍLIA

SERIES EDITOR'S FOREWORD

Simply Charly's *Great Lives* series offers concise yet deeply insightful introductions to the world's most influential thinkers and creators—scientists, artists, writers, economists, and other extraordinary figures whose ideas and achievements continue to shape our world.

Each book opens a window into the life and mind of its subject: their work, their inspirations, the pivotal moments that defined them, and the obstacles they overcame along the way. You'll also find glimpses of their lesser-known sides—the quirks, contradictions, and private battles that make geniuses feel unmistakably human.

Written by leading scholars and experts who have spent years studying their subjects, these volumes move far beyond the familiar timeline of "greatest hits." They dive deep into the thought processes, struggles, and turning points that propelled these figures toward their most enduring contributions.

The *Great Lives* series brings clarity and depth to complex lives, transforming historical icons into vivid, relatable individuals whose ambitions and doubts mirror our own.

Ultimately, we hope that these books do more than inform—that they inspire. Because the best stories of extraordinary lives don't just teach us about the past; they remind us what's possible in our own.

Charles Carlini
Publisher

PREFACE

John Maynard Keynes (1883-1946) was the most influential economist of the mid-20th century: he changed the way the world thought about economic problems and how those problems could be solved. For around 30 years after World War II, it was widely believed that, by using Keynesian theories, it was possible for governments to manage the economy to achieve full employment, avoiding the mass unemployment that had scarred the inter-war period. Maintaining approximately full employment and securing rapid economic growth helped create European welfare states, and the United States became what the economist and popular writer, John Kenneth Galbraith, called "the affluent society." Keynes was so influential that it became common to refer to these three decades as "The Age of Keynes" or "The Keynesian Era." Keynesianism was not just an economic theory or even a set of policy prescriptions: it became a social and political philosophy.

As we now know, this era was not to last. In the 1970s, following the emergence of "stagflation"—simultaneously rising inflation and unemployment—there was a reaction against Keynesian economics. Milton Friedman converted many people to "monetarism"—the doctrine that the main factor determining the rate of inflation is the growth rate of the money supply—with his argument that trying to stabilize the economy at a high level of employment would be counterproductive, as it would be liable to produce accelerating inflation. Together with Friedrich Hayek, who had been prominent in the 1930s and who rose from obscurity after he was awarded the Nobel Memorial Prize in Economic Sciences in 1974, Friedman persuaded many policymakers that government intervention typically made things worse and that governments should abandon any attempt to manage the level of demand: instead of discretionary monetary and fiscal policy aimed at maintaining full employment, governments should adopt a rigid rule for the growth rate of the money supply. When Friedman's monetary rule turned out to be problematic, many governments did not return to Keynesian demand management but adopted inflation targets, with central banks being mandated to follow policy rules. By the end of the 20th century, Keynesianism appeared to be dead.

The global financial crisis of 2008 challenged this approach. It was not the first financial crisis to emerge since the turn to so-called free markets—there had been a major crisis in East Asia, and there had been a spectacular "dot com" bubble that had burst—but unlike earlier crises, the one in 2008 threatened to bring down the whole world's financial system and, with it, cause a return to mass unemployment not seen since the 1930s. Action needed to be taken, and there was a sudden flurry of interest in Keynesian ideas. Keynes seemed relevant once more. However, this surge of interest did not last long. Within a few years, worries about rising levels of government debt caused many governments to institute policies of "austerity," cutting back on government spending on the grounds that government debt was rising to unsustainable levels. (Increasing taxes, the other way to reduce a government deficit, was believed to undermine incentives to work and to invest, and was therefore not seen as an alternative.) Such policies were applied in the United States, Britain, and the Eurozone. Keynesian attempts to maintain full employment were abandoned.

Whatever your views on the merits of the policies pursued during this period, there is little doubt that Keynes was, for good or bad, one of the key figures in the 20th century. Unfortunately, this does not mean that he is widely understood. The obvious way to understand him is to read his magnum opus, *The General Theory of Employment, Interest, and Money*(1936), but this presents difficulties. Keynes was an excellent writer, and some passages in the book can be read by anyone. For example, his account, in Chapter 12, of how people behave in financial markets is easy to understand and resonates with our experience today. The vision, outlined in Chapter 24, of a world in which goods are no longer scarce is highly accessible and reflects values to which Keynes was deeply committed, even if it will strike many readers as naïve. However, the heart of the book is an argument about technical economics that is difficult for non-economists to follow. People were interested in the book because of its implications for policy, but this work says very little about policy. It was even very difficult for Keynes' fellow economists, for he was defining new concepts and arguing in a deeply unfamiliar way. Even his account of what he called "classical economics"—the orthodoxy against which he was rebelling—was presented in a novel and challenging way.

The difficulties do not end here. *The General Theory* appeared at a time when economists were increasingly turning to mathematical modeling. Instead of theorizing with primarily verbal reasoning and all the subtleties and ambiguities that this involved, they were increasingly constructing sets of equations from which results could be derived rigorously. Inevitably, when economists tried to make sense of the book, many of them turned to these new methods, which meant that Keynes' ideas had to be simplified. Keynes had used mathematics: he repeatedly discussed propensities, functions, schedules, and how they fit together; and on some pages, he used simple algebra. This was enough for many early readers of the book to see it as a work of mathematical economics. However, many of the most important ideas in the book were analyzed only verbally, the mathematics providing no more than a skeleton on which to hang an argument that went beyond what could be captured in the mathematics. This style of reasoning differed greatly from the much more formal mathematical economics that was becoming fashionable. The result was that, to make sense of *The General Theory*, economists had to translate Keynes' mixture of mathematical and verbal reasoning into complete mathematical models that could be analyzed with the degree of rigor that was coming to be expected. This raised whether these translations were faithful to Keynes' thinking: were the new interpretations placing his essential insights on more secure foundations, or were they abandoning his main ideas?

Debates over these questions continued throughout the Keynesian era.

A further reason for the confusion over Keynes' ideas is that they are politically charged. Physical theories rarely have political or ideological implications, but economic theories do. An economic theory might imply that we would be better off if the government did something or did not do something, but this may clash with views about what people think the role of government should be. Whether the state should be large or small is not just an economic question: it is also a political one. Political views have led both supporters and critics of Keynesian policies to distort his ideas, either trying to make them more attractive to their audience or trying to show why they are clearly wrong. Nuance and subtlety get lost. For example, conservatives often portray Keynes as a socialist, associating his ideas with the economic failures of communist societies, even though, as we shall see, he was throughout his life a committed liberal, in the traditional European sense of someone who attached great importance to freedom and to a market economy; he even became a friend of Hayek.

A further difference between economics and much of natural science is that economic ideas deal with everyday concepts that people know and believe they understand—incomes, prices, savings, and spending money. People have preconceived ideas about economic problems in a way not true of much natural science. If a physicist makes a claim about what goes on inside an atom, people may not understand, but the physicist does not need to confront preexisting ideas. In contrast, if an economist claims, for example, that rising government debt is not a serious problem, she has to engage with what people know about debt in their own lives: that if they borrow more than they can repay, they are creating problems for themselves. People often assume that what is true for them must also be true for the government. Keynesian economists have had to battle, repeatedly, against this assumption.

A deeper reason we have often misunderstood Keynes is that the world has changed enormously since the 1930s. The heyday of Keynesian thinking, in the 1950s and 1960s, was very different from the inter-war period in which Keynes lived and worked. In place of economic chaos and the rise of Hitler and Mussolini, there was rapid economic growth, and European democracies appeared to be securely established. In place of the breakdown in international relations of the interwar period, there was the European Economic Community, later to become the European Union, and numerous organizations working to bring about international cooperation: the International Monetary Fund, the World Trade Organization, the World Bank, the Organization for Economic Co-operation and Development, and the United Nations. Until the 1990s, the Communist bloc was separate, the specter of nuclear war casting a shadow over East-West relations. Given these changes, it is not surprising that Keynesianism was reinterpreted by each generation, adapted to the new circumstances. Keynesianism thus became more than the ideas of a single person: it became both an evolving body of economic theories and a worldview that inevitably parted company with that of its founder.

This is enough to tell us about the questions to which we need answers if we are to understand Keynes. We obviously need to ask "Who was Keynes?" and "What were the ideas that made such a mark on the 20th century?" However, in order to understand the significance of his ideas, we also need to understand Keynesianism as it emerged and evolved after his death. To do this, we need to think about why his ideas were so influential for such a long period and why many economists and policymakers eventually abandoned his concepts. Only then can we tackle the question that most readers probably think is the most important one: "What is the relevance of Keynes' ideas today?" Understanding the history of Keynesian economics will, hopefully, make it possible to avoid falling into some of the traps into which many interpreters of Keynes have fallen.

Roger Backhouse
Birmingham, United Kingdom

ACKNOWLEDGMENTS

I came into economics around 1970, when the Keynesian consensus was still intact, even if it was being increasingly strongly challenged. As a student, I was exposed not only to the standard textbook account of Keynes, but also to the more radical interpretations of economists Joan Robinson and Axel Leijonhufvud, whose *On Keynesian Economics and the Economics of Keynes* was inspiring economists to think about Keynes in new ways. It was then that I acquired my first copy of the *General Theory*. In the 1980s, I wrote briefly about Keynes in a series of histories of economics, and I edited a collection of early reviews of the *General Theory*. So Keynesian economics, and the interpretation of Keynes, have been a part of my mindset from the beginning. However, it was only in 2002, when invited to edit *The Cambridge Companion to Keynes* together with Bradley Bateman, that I took a more serious interest in Keynes. Once that book was published, we went on to write a series of articles and eventually a short book, *Capitalist Revolutionary*. I am indebted to him for helping shape the views that I have tried to express simply in this book, and for checking this text for errors. With the possible exception of some of the interpretations that Bradley Bateman and I worked out together, I make no claim to originality. In the text, sources are provided only for direct quotations. An indication of my main sources is given in the suggestions for further reading. I am grateful to Steven Medema for providing extensive comments on a previous draft.

INTRODUCTION

The central component of any explanation of Keynes is what he was trying to say in his magnum opus, *The General Theory*, published in 1936, and how this changed the way economic problems were conceived during the next decade—the events that came to be called "the Keynesian revolution." However, to understand Keynes and Keynesianism, we need to start at a much earlier point in Keynes' life, for his upbringing is crucial to comprehending who he was and why he was able to achieve what he did. A key to understanding his life and work is that he was both a rebel, challenging the orthodoxies of the day, and part of the establishment. Chapter 1 shows how he was able to get into that seemingly contrary position. It covers his upbringing, as the child of eminent Victorian parents, his education at Cambridge University, the important friendships he established there, and his rapid rise in Britain's economic establishment.

There were two aspects of Keynes' ideas that both

appealed to his supporters and offended his opponents. The first is that he clearly developed a new theory about how capitalism worked and why it sometimes failed to produce the results expected of it. The second is his argument that the government should do things that some believe it should not be doing. This was a moral position as much as an economic one, and it is pursued in Chapter 2, which focuses on what Keynes was doing in the 1920s. During this decade, he was thinking deeply about theoretical questions, but he was also strongly engaged in policy analysis using theoretical frameworks developed by the older generation of economists. He used standard economic theories, but he applied them in a new way. Keynes was not shy about accusing policymakers of moral as well as intellectual failings. Nowhere is that clearer than in the book that made his reputation, providing the basis for his fortune—his attack on the Versailles peace conference in 1919. This moral stance, urging policymakers to take responsibility for the consequences of their actions and to do things that would otherwise not get done, permeates his writings on monetary policy and unemployment. This attitude underlies virtually everything he wrote. It is the presumption on which his arguments in favor of the government doing something about unemployment rest, and to which anti-Keynesian economists such as Milton Friedman later objected on moral as well as on economic grounds.

Chapter 3 then turns to the theory Keynes developed in the 1930s to explain why unemployment could arise. It provides a straightforward account of what he was trying to do in the book, *The General Theory of Employment, Interest and Money*, on which his current reputation rests, and of the main ideas found in the book. By focusing on the big picture, the chapter tries to avoid most of the controversies in which economists have since become entangled when discussing Keynes' ideas.

One of the features of Keynes' career is that he was not a conventional academic economist. He was a Fellow of King's College, Cambridge, and he gave a course of lectures in Cambridge each year. After 1919, however, he supported himself financially by writing articles for newspapers and magazines, as well as working in the City of London for banks and an insurance company. Chapter 3 argues that in several parts of his seminal work, Keynes was reflecting on this experience in a way that made his work different from that of many other academic economists. His writing also contains clear signs of his involvement with his artistic friends in the Bloomsbury Group.

Keynes' *General Theory* is then viewed from a different perspective in Chapter 4, which examines how economists responded to the book, not only in Britain but also in the United States and the rest of the world. The focus shifts from what Keynes thought he was doing to how other people interpreted what he had written. They took what they believed to be the key ideas found in the book and refashioned them according to the problems they were dealing with. The reaction of American economists to *The General Theory* is particularly important because, after World War II, the United States was the dominant power in the world, economically, politically, and intellectually (except, of course, in the Communist bloc). Breaking out only a few years after the publication of Keynes' book, World War II was crucial because, although designed to explain depression, Keynes' ideas proved invaluable for analyzing wartime problems of scarce resources and potential inflation. During the war, even Milton Friedman conceded that Keynes' approach to analyzing the economy was useful. After the war ended, the economic situation and the problems with which economists were concerned changed again.

The shifting political and economic climate was not the only reason that Keynesian ideas needed to be continually reinterpreted. During the 1930s, long before Keynes' book appeared, economists were tackling economics in new ways, making greater use of mathematics. Mathematical economics was still a minority activity in that many economists clung to earlier approaches involving purely verbal reasoning, but interest in using mathematics to theorize more rigorously was growing rapidly, and by the 1960s, it had clearly become the dominant approach to economic theory. Naturally, economists sought to interpret Keynesian theory using these new methods, constructing mathematical models that they claimed were more rigorous accounts of Keynes' ideas. This development of Keynesian theories happened alongside attempts to use his ideas to guide policy, some of the new models being designed explicitly to provide the advice that politicians and government officials needed. As was explained earlier, policymakers were now using Keynesian ideas under circumstances that differed greatly from those in which Keynes had developed his concepts. Without getting into technical details, Chapter 4 outlines this development, explaining why, even in the 1970s, 40 years *after The General Theory*, and three decades after Keynes' death, this process of reinterpreting Keynesian theory was still ongoing.

In order to understand Keynesian economics, we also need to grasp why economists and many of those responsible for the conduct of nations' economic affairs turned against Keynes so much that some economists saw Keynesianism as dead, believing that its theories had been based on naïve and discredited assumptions about human behavior. This is the subject of Chapter 5. Just as there had been different elements in Keynesianism, this theory was attacked in different ways. Milton Friedman, whose objections to Keynes were moral or political as much as economic, provided a highly influential critique: whereas Keynes had faith in the ability of government to improve the way society worked, Friedman and many of his associates did not. Government, they believed, typically made problems worse. Other economic theorists and statisticians argued that Keynesian models did not work because this approach was conceptually flawed. The economic chaos that erupted in the 1970s gave these critiques much of their traction.

As had been the case with the rise of Keynesianism, war was again crucial. Problems began with the Vietnam War, the cost of which escalated in the late 1960s and early 1970s. Given that President Lyndon Johnson was unwilling to scale back his Great Society program—far-reaching policies of national reform—and either could not or would not raise taxes, the result was an increase in aggregate demand. By 1970, the rate of inflation had already gone up, but events came to a head in 1973 after the Yom Kippur War between Israel and its Arab neighbors, when the Organization of Petroleum Exporting Countries massively increased the price of oil, and an embargo was placed on supplying oil to countries that had supported Israel. Even though the immediate cause of the crisis was an unprecedented event, critics claimed that, even if Keynesianism had been appropriate in the 1950s and 1960s (and that was disputed), it could no longer provide useful policy guidance, and its theoretical foundations were considered suspect.

By the beginning of the 21st century, economists were speaking of a "Great Moderation." It was widely believed that the business cycle was now under control, not because of Keynesian policies but due to liberalization, deregulation, removing barriers to international trade, and, above all, by giving central banks independence so that setting interest rates would no longer be driven by short-term political considerations. However, as Chapter 6 explains, this optimistic vision was shattered by the global financial crisis of 2008, when even economists who had never previously studied Keynes took his ideas seriously. As the specter of another Great Depression loomed in 2008-2009, anxious policymakers suddenly turned to Keynes. Yet again, Keynesianism had to be reinterpreted. When interest rates fell to zero, central banks lost much of their ability to stimulate the economy, raising the possibility, pretty much ignored since the 1930s, that the world might be faced with the prospect of long-term stagnation.

The book ends with some suggestions on the relevance of Keynes for today. Up to this point, I have been approaching Keynes and Keynesianism as a historian, trying to explain what happened without taking sides. In the last chapter, my position changes to that of an economist, expressing an opinion, informed by history, on what should happen. I argue that, even if Keynes' ideas are still relevant (as I think they are), they need to be reinterpreted for the modern world. As the final chapter argues, this was a position that Keynes himself would have endorsed. Indeed, some confusion over Keynesian economics has arisen because economists have lost sight of this, trying to find a single "true" Keynesian doctrine, valid for all times and places. Hopefully, this book will have shown that Keynesian ideas have been so powerful because different generations have creatively reworked them.

1
SERIOUS ABOUT TRUTH AND BEAUTY

A CHILD OF THE VICTORIAN ERA

John Maynard Keynes, who always went by the name of Maynard, was born in 1883, the son of two outstanding representatives of the Victorian era. His mother, Florence Keynes, was active in good works and was the first woman to be elected mayor of Cambridge, where they lived. His father, John Neville Keynes, was an economist at Cambridge University. He was the author of a somewhat dry textbook, *The Scope and Method of Political Economy* (1891), that students were told to read but probably did not. The senior Keynes became a major figure in university administration, rising to be Registrary, an old-fashioned title (unique to Cambridge) for the senior administrative officer, a position he held from 1910 to 1925. As one would expect of any such upper-middle-class family, they made ample provision for Maynard's education, sending him first to Eton (one of the country's top private schools), where he excelled, and then to Cambridge, where he held a scholarship to King's College.

Keynes was later to rebel against the values of the Victorian era, many of which were amply represented by his parents. However, he learned much from them that was important to his subsequent career. His first biographer, Roy Harrod, referred to the "presuppositions of Harvey Road," the location of the comfortable and substantial house that the family moved to around the time of Maynard's birth.* These presuppositions included a belief in the stability of the British Empire and the society that went with it. Keynes was later to reject this assumption, but there was another commonly-held notion he never rejected and which formed the basis of much of what he did: a strong sense of duty—a social conscience—and a belief that the educated classes had a responsibility to do what they could to solve the problems facing society. Keynes was a member of an intellectual elite, but for him, as for his parents, this position in society came with obligations as well as privileges.

This sense of duty was also central to the thinking of one of the dominant figures in the intellectual world in which Keynes grew up: Henry Sidgwick, a family friend and close associate of Neville Keynes. Maynard knew him well. He was an important figure in Cambridge, playing a major role in modernizing the university, notably in helping establish Newnham College for women. In the late 19th century, traditional religious beliefs were being questioned as a result of historical scholarship and challenges from science. Sidgwick addressed these issues more rigorously than most of his contemporaries, at one point even deciding that he

---

* Harrod, The Life of John Maynard Keynes (1951), 4-5.

needed to learn Near Eastern languages in order to get into the mindset out of which Christianity had emerged, a commitment to rigor that Keynes could not understand. Like many intellectuals of his generation, Sidgwick lost his Christian faith. In the 1850s, Cambridge, like Oxford, was only part of the way through the transition from being an institution that trained Church of England clergy to a modern research university; college Fellows were still required to subscribe to the 39 articles of the Church of England. Sidgwick's conscience forced him to resign rather than, like many others in his situation, make a profession in which he did not believe. He regained his Fellowship soon after when the rules were relaxed.

No longer bound by religious belief, was there still a place for ethics and morality? This was the question that obsessed Sidgwick for the rest of his life. He wrote major treatises on political economy—the name by which the discipline we call economics was known for most of the 19th century—and on politics, but his most important work was *The Methods of Ethics* (1874). As its title makes clear, this book was not about defining ethical behavior: it was about working out the principles on which ethics could be based. He spent his life trying to make the case for utilitarianism—the notion derived from Jeremy Bentham and John Stuart Mill—that what mattered was the greatest happiness of the greatest number of people. Sidgwick wanted to prove that this rule should govern life, but he never managed to solve the problem.

Though Keynes and his friends believed they were moving on from Sidgwick's views—they saw him as a representative of their parents' generation—they had more in common with him than they acknowledged. Keynes never accepted Sidgwick's utilitarian ethics, but he shared his commitment to working out a coherent moral position. More importantly, it is far from clear that he rejected utilitarianism as a political philosophy. In his biography of the young Keynes, Robert Skidelsky has written,

> Keynes's life was balanced between two sets of moral claims. His duty as an individual was to achieve good states of mind for himself and for those he was directly concerned with; his duty as a citizen was to help achieve a happy state of affairs for society. The two claims he thought of as logically independent of each other. ... He was as timid about his expectations of realizing good states of mind on a large scale as he was bold in his expectations about the amount of happiness or utility a government could deliver. ... The duty of the state was to realise happiness.*

At this time, economics in Cambridge was part of the Moral Sciences Tripos, a field covered by Sidgwick's major books *The Methods of Ethics, Principles of Political Economy* (1883), and *Elements of Politics* (1891) (the tripos refers to the three Parts of the undergraduate degree, though confusingly, it was normal for students to take just Parts I and II). It was not yet the separate, technical discipline that it became in the 20th century. The person responsible for initiating that change in Cambridge was not Sidgwick but Alfred Marshall, whose ideas were responsible for shaping Cambridge economics, and indeed economics in much of

---

* Skidelsky, John Maynard Keynes, Volume 1: Hopes Betrayed, 1883-1920 (1983), 157.

the English-speaking world, until his death in 1924. A close associate of Sidgwick in the 1860s, Marshall's initial interests were in philosophy and psychology, all part of the Moral Sciences tripos. Because Fellows were not allowed to marry, Marshall left Cambridge in 1877 when he married, becoming Principal of University College, Bristol. After a year at Oxford, he returned to Cambridge in 1884 as Professor of Political Economy. In 1890, he published his *Principles of Economics*, a textbook that came to dominate the English-speaking world. Though he was a mathematician who had derived much of his theory using mathematics, Marshall was suspicious of mathematics and presented his theory in ordinary language, buttressed by diagrams. The center of his theory was how the prices and quantities of goods were determined by supply and demand. The basic hypothesis was very simple and could be presented in a diagram comprising a supply curve and a demand curve. However, rather than develop the mathematics, Marshall provided a verbal account of how markets would operate over different time periods. In the shortest of periods, supply was whatever had been produced, so price would depend on how scarce the goods in question were. If more time were available, firms could respond to price changes by increasing or reducing production. In the long run, they would be able to adopt new production techniques, install new machinery, and build new factories (or they could get rid of unwanted capital), enabling production to respond even further to changes in demand conditions.

Crucially for Keynes, Marshall also developed a version of the so-called quantity theory of money. To understand this, it is crucial to comprehend the distinction between money and income. Income is measured as a flow—it is the amount of money received in a unit of time. This means that income could be expressed as $10,000 a month, or $120,000 a year; they are the same. The length of time is crucial. In contrast, money is the amount of money someone has at a particular moment: think of it as the amount you have in the bank on December 31, or at the end of each month. Holding more money than another person does not necessarily mean you are wealthier. It could be that, although you have more money in the bank, the other person has a higher income and can sustain a higher standard of living. Or it could be that you have decided to keep your savings in the bank (which counts as money, usually defined as cash in circulation with the public plus bank deposits), whereas someone else has chosen to buy shares or invest in a house, assets which are forms of wealth but do not count as money.

The quantity theory of money states that there is a relationship between the quantity of money in circulation (the stock of money) and the average price of goods and services or, equivalently, a relationship between the growth rate of the money supply and the rate of inflation (the rate of change of the price level). The quantity theory has a long history, going back at least to the influx of gold and silver into Europe after the Spanish conquest of the Americas in the 15th and 16th centuries. The theory was later developed by John Locke in the 17th century and by David Hume in the 18th. By the early 20th century, though it was interpreted in different ways, it was the standard theory of the price level.

According to Marshall's version of the theory, people desire to hold a certain fraction of their resources as money. Because of this, there would be a relationship between the value of goods and services being produced and the amount of money that people wish to hold. Equilibrium requires that people want to hold the amount of money in existence because, if people had more money than they wanted to hold, they would increase their spending, and if they were holding less than they wanted, they would spend less in order to replenish their money balances. Putting this together, you get the result that if, for some reason, there was an increase in the quantity of money, there must eventually be an increase in the value of goods and services. Given that the physical quantity of goods and services was determined by "real" factors—the availability of labor, machinery, and raw materials—this meant that prices would have to rise. In the long run, a doubling of the money supply must eventually lead to a doubling of the price level, and a halving of the money supply must lead to a halving of the price level.

However, in the short run, a rise in the money supply would increase production: more money in circulation would lead to higher spending, raising prices first, increasing profit margins, and causing production to expand; this, in turn, would raise demand for labor and raw materials, causing wages and costs to go up as well. As costs rose, eventually catching up with the spike in prices, profit margins would be restored to their original level, causing output to fall back to its normal level. There would therefore be fluctuations in output, but they would be only temporary, and there was no reason to believe that unemployment (then a novel term, first used in 1896) would be long-term. This was one of the doctrines that Keynes was eventually to challenge.

TRUTH, BEAUTY, AND FRIENDSHIP

In the 19th century, King's College was an extension of Eton, the best students progressing almost seamlessly from one to the other. Keynes arrived at King's in 1902, after a brilliant career at Eton, with a four-year scholarship—ample time to finish his degree and prepare himself for his future career. He did not study economics but took the examinations in mathematics, though, to the dismay of his father, he regularly took time away from mathematics to pursue his literary, political, and philosophical interests.

As Sidgwick had done a generation earlier, Keynes joined a semi-secret society known as the Apostles. This was an undergraduate group that took itself seriously, meeting to debate difficult moral issues. The dominant influence on Keynes' generation was the philosopher G. E. Moore, whose *Principia Ethica* was published in 1903, the year after Keynes' arrival at King's. The foundation of Moore's ethics was the notion that people perceived goodness such as it is. Something was not good because of something else, such as its ability to bring pleasure: it was simply good in and by itself, and one recognized intuitively what was good and what was not. This was a philosophy to which Keynes subscribed. However, although the Apostles took themselves very seriously, as people of their age are wont to do, this did not preclude having fun. On the contrary, Moore taught that the highest ends in life were art, beauty, and friendship. Many of Keynes' friends also saw homosexuality as a high aim. Keynes was a practicing homosexual (which was illegal, and for which people could be sent to prison) until he shocked his friends by falling in love with the Russian ballerina, Lydia Lopokova, who came to London with Sergei Diaghilev's ballet company, and whom he married in 1925.

Keynes was also heavily involved in politics while a student. This was a time of the "new Liberalism," in which the British Liberal Party—the party of the eminent Victorian statesman, William Gladstone—was being pulled in a more collectivist direction. The Labour Party had been formed a decade earlier, but was still very small, and Labour representatives were generally elected to parliament as Liberals. As a student, Keynes was active in the Liberal Club and regularly took part in debates in the Cambridge Union. He was a Liberal Imperialist, viewing the British Empire as a force for good, encouraging free trade and self-government in the colonies. On domestic issues, his politics were to the left, supporting moderate measures of social reform and redistribution of income.

Keynes' father followed his progress closely, and while his lack of attention to mathematics was a cause for great concern and anxiety, Maynard did not neglect mathematics altogether. When he took his examinations, he achieved first-class honors, although he was only 12th in the ranking of candidates for the degree. This was a position he had predicted accurately, though it dismayed his father, who believed he was capable of more.

Keynes never obtained a degree or any other formal qualification in economics, and it was only after his graduation that he had any systematic instruction on the subject. The reason was that he had decided to enter the Civil Service examinations, and economics was one of the required subjects. He had, of course, absorbed much knowledge of the field from Sidgwick and Marshall, whom he knew well, and through extensive reading at home, but further preparation was needed. To prepare for the examination, he spent two months studying economics under Marshall's tutelage. This was a highly intensive study, for during these two months, he wrote no fewer than 19 essays, each of which was the basis for a discussion with Marshall. Marshall thought highly of Keynes' work, considering two of his papers publishable. He took the examinations and came second. Unfortunately, there was only a single vacancy at the Treasury that year, so he was unable to work there; instead, he took up a position in the India Office, the institution responsible for managing relations with the region that was critical to the British Empire.

When Keynes was a student, the Boer War in South Africa had just ended, and questions of trade and the empire dominated British politics. In 1903, Joseph Chamberlain, a former Liberal politician who had switched to the Conservative Party, established the Tariff Reform League, which argued for strengthening the empire through a system of preferential tariffs. The belief was that, by establishing the empire as a trading zone protected by tariffs, Britain could compete more effectively with the much larger United States. Tariffs would also provide revenues that would pay for social reforms. This was a major departure from the policy of free trade to which Britain had been firmly committed, and tariff reformers were thus pitted against supporters of free trade. Marshall usually avoided controversy in his attempt to establish economics as a solid, scientific discipline, but even he became drawn into the debate, trying to bring the authority of economics to bear on the side of free trade. The attempt backfired in that it revealed that economists were split down the middle on the issue. Keynes became involved in campaigns in Cambridge on the

Liberal Imperialist side. He was to remain closely associated with the Liberal Party throughout his career.

The policy of tariff reform split the Conservative Party and was behind the landslide victory of the Liberal Party in 1906, which led to one of the great reforming governments of the 20th century. The reforms introduced included progressive income tax, old-age pensions, and unemployment insurance. From 1908, it was headed by Herbert Asquith, but it also included two figures who were to dominate British politics and hence Keynes' career for the next 40 years: David Lloyd George and Winston Churchill.

JOINING THE ESTABLISHMENT

In 1906, Keynes left Cambridge and moved to London, where he settled down in the area known as Bloomsbury, living with a group of friends he had made in Cambridge, mostly through the Apostles. He remained in this circle for the rest of his life. At the center of the group were Vanessa Bell and Virginia Woolf, daughters of the eminent Victorian writer, Leslie Stephen. It also included artists, such as Clive Bell and Duncan Grant, as well as writers—Leonard Woolf, Lytton Strachey, and E. M. Forster. Much of their inspiration came from the art critic Roger Fry, slightly older but part of the group nevertheless. They represented the values Keynes had learned from Moore and his friends in Cambridge, according to which friendship, art, and beauty were the highest values in life. Living communally, they were rebels against what they saw as the stuffiness of the Victorian age, portrayed very clearly in Virginia Woolf's novels and in Lytton Strachey's *Eminent Victorians* (1918).

This book presented generally unflattering portraits of

four revered Victorian figures: Cardinal Manning, Florence Nightingale, Thomas Arnold, and General Gordon. For example, Florence Nightingale, who revolutionized the treatment of casualties in the Crimean War, was portrayed not as the saintly "lady of the lamp" but as a ruthlessly efficient administrator, difficult to get along with, and who exploited her contacts in high places to get what she wanted. And hers was arguably the most favorable of all the portraits. General Gordon was depicted not as the heroic defender of Khartoum, but as a maverick mercenary soldier who got the British government into an impossible situation. As we shall see, Keynes was later to echo this debunking of the Victorian era and Strachey's iconoclastic style in his writing on economics. Like Strachey, Keynes had a strong interest in human psychology, and he wrote many biographical essays, 39 of which were later collected in a single volume, *Essays in Biography*. There was a great variety, his subjects including contemporary political figures, economists (including Thomas Robert Malthus, famous for his theory of population, and Marshall, Keynes' teacher), his friends, and a few scientists (Newton and Einstein).

Keynes shared the values of his Bloomsbury friends and their commitment to art, and as soon as his circumstances permitted, he supported them by buying their works and becoming a patron of the arts. After his marriage, he founded the Arts Theatre in Cambridge as a stage on which Lydia could perform, and towards the end of his life, he was a significant figure in founding the Arts Council, the government body that sponsored the arts in Britain. But what did this have to do with being an economist and a worldly one at that? Not only was Keynes outstanding at analyzing the economic world, but he also excelled at money-making, even if sometimes he nearly lost everything. He became Bursar of King's College, responsible for its finances, eventually making it one of the richest colleges in Cambridge. And he managed investments for a syndicate of his friends. So, how could he justify being more worldly than his Bloomsbury friends thought proper? The answer is that, unlike many economists, Keynes was skeptical about the morality of making money for its own sake; to him, there were higher goals in life. But money-making made artistic and literary pursuits possible. Economics was not an end in itself but a means to an end.

Keynes lived with his friends in Bloomsbury, but his work was in the India Office, where he became an expert on the financial relations between Britain and its colonies. This was a complex issue. One of the reasons for this was that payments made by India to Britain were seen by Whitehall as charges to meet costs incurred in administering the subcontinent, but considered by Indian nationalists as extracting tribute from a colony. A major complication was introduced by the fact that the Pound Sterling was tied to gold—the famous Gold Standard, which was to play a major role in British policy-making in the 1920s—whereas the Indian Rupee was tied to silver. This meant that changes in the prices of gold and silver led to changes in the exchange rate between the Sterling and the Rupee, affecting the balance of trade between the two countries and the value of payments from one to the other. Keynes acquired a reputation as one of the few people who understood all of this. The result of his experiences was his first book, with the self-explanatory title, *Indian Currency and Finance* (1913). In the same year, he served on a Royal Commission on Indian Finance and Currency. He had begun his career as it would eventually end, as a specialist in international monetary economics.

By the time the book came out, he had already left the India Office. In 1908, after only two years as a civil servant, he returned to Cambridge. He had learned much from working, but the life of a Civil Servant was not for him. He found his job boring and wanted to engage in scientific and theoretical work.

Returning to Cambridge was a slightly risky step, which his father opposed because, at this point, Maynard had no college position, crucial for a secure career in Cambridge. His goal was a Fellowship at King's, but even this would initially be for a limited period, and it was highly competitive, involving the submission of a dissertation. His dissertation was on the theory of probability. Given the way his ideas developed in the 1930s, it is tempting to suppose that this flowed from his interest in economics, but that temptation should be resisted, for his work on probability arose out of his thinking about ethics. The fellowship dissertation was a work in philosophy, not economics.

The ideas behind Keynes' work on probability dated back at least to an earlier paper, "Ethics in relation to conduct," the precise dating of which is uncertain. (It may have been a paper presented to the Apostles in 1904, when he was still an undergraduate, though some evidence indicates a later date.) Keynes argued that for conduct to be rational, we must have reason to believe that our actions will probably produce good; we need to have reason to believe that one action will probably produce more good than another. This required not only an understanding of good, but also an understanding of probability. Moore had argued that good was a primitive concept that one simply recognized: it was a concept that was not reducible to anything else. Keynes applied similar reasoning to probabilities. Probabilities were degrees of belief—a primitive notion that could not be reduced to anything else, such as the frequencies with which different events were observed. It was therefore impossible to explain why probabilities took the values that they did, any more than it was possible to say why certain things were good. The concept of probability was objective and recognized directly by intuition. The theory of probability was, therefore, an exercise in logic.

Keynes first submitted his dissertation in December 1907, but there were few fellowships available, and he was successful only on his second attempt a year later. Working on it in his spare time, the dissertation was eventually published in 1921 as *A Treatise on Probability*. By then, much else had happened, and his situation had been transformed.

His initial position in Cambridge was as a lecturer, one of two posts paid for by A. C. Pigou, who had just been appointed Professor at Marshall's retirement. Naturally, Keynes lectured on monetary economics about which he had learned so much in the India Office. He also became closely involved with the Royal Economic Society and its journal, both of which Marshall had been instrumental in founding, becoming both Secretary of the Society and Editor of the *Economic Journal* in 1911. He held these positions until his death 35 years later. He was assisted in the latter role for several years by his predecessor, Francis Edgeworth, Professor of Economics at Oxford, who had edited the journal since its founding in 1891, and in the 1920s and 1930s by two other colleagues, but he was nonetheless an active editor, reading submissions and making decisions on what would be published, often without taking advice from external referees, as would be normal practice today. For the first four years, he could not even charge the cost of secretarial assistance to the Society. Like Edgeworth, he had no inhibitions about publishing his own work in the journal or publishing comments on other people's articles.

On August 4, 1914, Britain declared war on Germany. In the days leading up to that event, the solvency of the financial system had been threatened by a banking crisis, which arose from Britain's position in the world trading system. Defaults by foreign creditors caused short-term money markets to stop functioning, and commercial banks turned to the Bank of England for gold, even though they stopped issuing gold to their customers. The Bank of England's gold reserves fell rapidly from £17.5 million to £11 million, and so a bank holiday was declared for three days. Keynes, who had recently been working on such matters with the Royal Commission on Indian Finance and Currency, was immediately summoned to the Treasury to provide advice. When he received the letter, on a Sunday, he did not even wait for the next train to London; he persuaded his brother-in-law to take him there in the sidecar of his motorcycle, walking the last stretch of the journey along Whitehall, to preserve some dignity on his arrival. This enabled him to arrive before any decision had been taken. It is believed that his memorandum persuaded the Prime Minister, David Lloyd George, to maintain the convertibility of Sterling into gold for as long as possible, and he was involved in discussions about how to get the financial system working again.

He eventually got a position in the Treasury at the beginning of 1915, though retaining his connection to Cambridge through his Fellowship at King's College and continuing to edit the *Economic Journal*. It was a junior position, but it placed Keynes near the top of government. Early on, he served as secretary of a Cabinet Committee chaired by the Prime Minister, and he accompanied Lloyd George as an economic advisor at a conference in France that established the system of wartime lending between the nations fighting Germany. He became progressively more involved in government activities, rising rapidly within the Treasury.

Initially, Keynes took little interest in the politics of the war. He was not caught up in the wave of patriotism that accompanied the start of the war, but neither was he strongly opposed to the war. It was only later that the horrors of the war became clear. He eventually tried to register as a conscientious objector, supporting friends who did the same, an action that he did not need to do because, as a Treasury official, he was exempt from military service. The reason Keynes gave was not a moral opposition to the war, but that he objected to the state deciding on his behalf—this was the position of someone who attached great importance to freedom.

2

A MORAL RESPONSIBILITY TO INTERVENE

VERSAILLES—A MORAL FAILURE

Keynes ended the war as a senior official in the Treasury who was intimately connected to Cambridge economics, still the heart of the British economics Establishment (by 1918, the London School of Economics, founded in 1895, had not yet developed to the point where it could challenge Cambridge's dominance). However, many of his attitudes, like those of his Bloomsbury friends, were those of an outsider and iconoclast. Keynes was concerned with morality and refused to accept the conventional order, a view represented by Strachey's debunking of four eminent Victorians. In the years that followed, Keynes repeatedly brought moral arguments to bear on issues of economic policy, which he never treated merely as technical economic problems.

The first context in which we can see this is *Economic Consequences of the Peace*, published in 1919. One of the problems to emerge at the Peace Conference, which began at

Versailles in January 1919, was the gap between the reparations demanded by the Allied governments and what some believed Germany would be able to pay. He became exhausted by the negotiations, and by May, upon learning that the overall settlement would, in his opinion, place unbearable burdens on Germany, he had decided to resign rather than be a party to an agreement he believed both unworkable and immoral. By June, he had written a book about what had happened, on which he worked over the summer, and which was published in December. It became a best-seller and made his reputation, laying the foundation on which he could later build a fortune. Robert Skidelsky, one of his biographers, has described this as the best book Keynes ever wrote because it reveals so many of his different talents.

The book opened with a chapter on the economic situation in Europe before the war. Since 1870, a complex trading system had developed, in which the countries of Europe had become dependent on each other. Particularly important was the large dependence of many nations on trade with Germany. In addition, Europe, with its large population, relied on the United States for food. These supplies were in danger as the US needed more and more of its resources to feed its own people.

During the same period, Europe had accumulated vast wealth. The savings that made this possible had taken place only because wealth was unequally distributed: the working class was unable to consume much because they owned little, and the capitalist class, though free to consume, chose not to do so because they believed they had a duty to save.

> The duty of 'saving' became nine-tenths of virtue and the growth of the cake the object of true religion. There grew around the non-consumption of the cake all those instincts of puritanism which in other ages has withdrawn itself from the world and has neglected the arts of production as well as those of enjoyment.*

The war, Keynes contended, shattered the illusions on which this equilibrium was based: it had "disclosed the possibility of consumption to all and the vanity of abstinence to many." He continued,

> Thus the bluff is discovered; the labouring classes may be no longer willing to forgo so largely, and the capitalist classes, no longer confident of the future, may seek to enjoy more fully their liberties of consumption so long as they last, and thus precipitate the hour of their confiscation.†

When we look back at these passages, knowing how Keynes' ideas were to develop later, they are remarkable. He was providing an account of what was going on in the world, but in doing so, he was also passing a clear judgment on the morals of the Victorian era. For over a century, economists have focused on the link between saving and growth. Saving was the way assets increased, and capital accumulation was the key to economic growth. This argument, combined with a puritan suspicion of luxury consumption,

---

* Economic Consequences of the Peace, The Collected Writings of John Maynard Keynes, vol. II (hereafter ECP) 12.

† ECP, 13.

made the moral case for saving. Keynes accepted the link between saving and economic growth, but using a social-psychological argument, he challenged the moral case for saving, reaching very different conclusions from those of policymakers trying to return to the pre-war world. Throughout his career, he was concerned with saving and investment, developing new ways to comprehend them. And although his focus was on understanding how the world worked, the moral issues surrounding saving and investment were never far from his mind.

After describing Europe's situation before the war, Keynes turned to the Versailles conference itself, focusing on psychological portraits of the four leading participants and their motives. George Clemenceau, the President of France, was crucial; his ideas effectively framed the subsequent treaty. "He felt about France what Pericles felt of Athens—unique value in her, nothing else mattering; but his theory of politics was Bismarck's. He had one illusion—France; and one disillusion—mankind, including Frenchmen, and his colleagues not least," Keynes wrote about him.* More hope was pinned on the American President, Woodrow Wilson, an academic who delivered The Fourteen Points speech to Congress in 1918, where he outlined his vision for ending the war. He was, according to Keynes,

> a generously intentioned man, with many of the weaknesses of other human beings, and lacking that dominating equipment which would have been necessary to cope with the subtle and dangerous spellbinders whom a tremendous clash of forces and personalities had brought

---

* ECP, 20.

to the top as triumphant masters in the swift game of give and take, face to face in council—a game of which he had no experience at all.*

As for his temperament,

The President was like a nonconformist minister, perhaps a Presbyterian. His thought and his temperament were essentially theological, not intellectual, with all the strength and weakness of that manner of thought, feeling, and expression.

Wilson had come to the conference with admirable principles, but he had not fleshed them out, falling victim to the guile of the British Prime Minister, David Lloyd George.

What chance could such a man have against Mr. Lloyd George's unerring, almost medium-like, sensibility to everyone immediately round him? To see the British Prime Minister watching the company, with six or seven senses not available to ordinary men, judging character, motive, and subconscious impulse, perceiving what each was thinking and even what each was going to say next, and compounding with telepathic instinct the argument or appeal best suited to the vanity, weakness, or self-interest of his immediate auditor, was to realise that the poor President would be playing blind man's bluff in that party.†

In paragraphs not included in the book because Keynes

* ECP, 24.

† ECP, 25-26.

was not happy with them (perhaps they went too far, given that he was referring to a friend and colleague), he described Lloyd George as a '*femme fatale*'—"this siren, this goat-dotted bard, this half-human visitor to our age from the hag-ridden magic and enchanted woods of Celtic antiquity."[*] The result was that the drama centered on "An old man of the world, a *femme fatale*, and a non-conformist clergyman."[†] It was a vivid description of the conference that only someone who had been an insider could have written. By analyzing the psychology of the main actors, Keynes explained how the terms of the treaty emerged, summarizing the outcome in a short paragraph:

> The thoughts which I have expressed in the second chapter [on pre-war Europe] were not present to the mind of Paris. The future life of Europe was not their concern; its means of livelihood was not their anxiety. Their preoccupations, good and bad alike, related to frontiers and nationalities, to the balance of power, to imperial aggrandisements, to the future enfeeblement of a strong and dangerous enemy, to revenge, and to the shifting by the victors of their unbearable financial burdens on to the shoulders of the defeated.[‡]

Keynes then turned to an analysis of the terms of the treaty, drawing on detailed statistics on international trade and finance. He concluded Germany could not pay the reparations demanded because the means by which they could

---

* Eventually published as Essays in Biography, The Collected Writings of John Maynard Keynes, vol. X (hereafter EB), 23.

† EB, 22.

‡ ECP, 35.

be paid were being removed: Germany's merchant fleet had been taken away, and important territories, including coal-fields crucial to industry, had been ceded to other countries. Readers might not understand all the technical arguments about Germany's ability to pay, but they would be able to grasp the argument that the treaty was immoral.

> The policy of reducing Germany to servitude for a generation, of degrading the lives of millions of human beings, and of depriving a whole nation of happiness should be abhorrent and detestable—abhorrent and detestable, even if it were possible, even if it enriched ourselves, even if it did not sow the decay of the whole civilised life of Europe. Some preach it in the name of justice. In the great events of man's history, in the unwitting of the complex fates of nations, justice is not so simple. And if it were, nations are not authorised, by religion or natural morals, to visit on the children of their enemies the misdoings of parents or rulers.*

Keynes, therefore, proposed policies by which this potentially disastrous situation for Europe could be improved.

Economic Consequences of the Peace was important for Keynes personally, establishing him as a celebrity who could find an audience for his views. It revealed him to be a great writer, evidence for which is seen in some of the quotations used here. More than that, although the book contained no significant innovations in economic theory, it showed important features of Keynes' thinking. His style owed much

* ECP, 142.

to his friend, Lytton Strachey, and his denunciation of the pre-war world paralleled Strachey's debunking of the Victorian era. Economic policy was not just a technical activity and should never lose track of the moral implications of what was being done. This is a theme that we will explore in relation to his other work in the 1920s. With hindsight, informed by the evolution of Keynes' thinking in the 1930s, we can also attach importance to his deep, perhaps even emotional, concern with saving and investment, and to the importance he attached to the social psychology of the situations he was analyzing.

RETURNING TO THE GOLD STANDARD

Having resigned from the Treasury, Keynes had to think about his career. He still had his Fellowship at King's College, he was still editing the *Economic Journal*, and one option would have been to return to being a full-time academic. However, though he continued to be involved with King's, even becoming its Bursar, responsible for the College's financial affairs, encouraged by the success of *Economic Consequences of the Peace,* he supported himself by journalism. Also, he had made money through speculation and investments before the war, and these activities continued. He became involved in the City of London, becoming a director of a bank and an insurance company. The government still sought his advice, and he had the connections necessary to make his opinions known to the relevant people. He was not a conventional academic.

Two policy issues dominated Keynes' agenda during the 1920s. There was the ongoing controversy over reparations payments by Germany, on which there was a string of international conferences, renegotiating the terms of the treaty. He was heavily involved in discussing these issues. He updated *Economic Consequences of the Peace* with a new book, *A Revision of the Treaty* (1921). In the same year, Keynes negotiated with the *Manchester Guardian* newspaper to become the editor of a series of supplements on reconstruction in Europe. He aimed to influence policymakers. When the first of these supplements would not appear until 10 days after a conference in Genoa had started, he arranged for his proposals to be printed in a newspaper article in time to be taken into account by the participants, and he tried to get an early copy of the supplement for the Chancellor of the Exchequer, who was attending the meeting.

In a different type of intervention, he debated the technical theoretical arguments about the effect of reparations on German international trade with the Swedish economist, Bertil Ohlin, in the *Economic Journal*. The remarkable feature of this exchange is that Keynes was thinking about international trade in very traditional terms, reflecting his Marshallian background. He assumed that, in order to change trade flows, it was necessary for reparations to change international prices. In contrast, Ohlin argued the payments would reduce German incomes and raise revenues in Allied countries directly, even if prices did not change at all. The significance of this seemingly erudite point is that Ohlin was using an argument that was to become fundamental to the new theory that Keynes developed in the 1930s—that changes in income could produce changes in spending, even without changes in prices. It was an argument to which, in the 1920s, he was still blind.

The other main item on the policy agenda was Britain's exchange-rate policy. In 1717, Isaac Newton, the Master of the Mint, established a new parity between gold and silver, which led to a dramatic reduction in the amount of silver in circulation. From then on, Britain was on a gold standard, with the price of gold fixed at £3 17s. 10½d. per ounce of gold (there were 20 shillings in a pound and 12 pence in a shilling). This was the parity that had lasted, with an interruption during the wars that followed the French Revolution, for almost two centuries, during which Britain's power and wealth had risen enormously. It was the parity that Keynes had urged Lloyd George to support during the 1914 run on sterling. During the war, British prices rose more than American prices, and eventually, the government had to concede that the value of sterling in relation to gold and, crucially, in relation to the US dollar, needed to be reduced. However, once the war was over, the decision was made to return to the gold standard at the pre-war parity of $4.86 to the pound (equivalent to the gold price set by Newton). It was believed that this would restore confidence and contribute to a return to prosperity.

Keynes was convinced that this policy was mistaken. He believed that two factual mistakes underpinned the argument to return. During the war, price rises had made British goods uncompetitive at the old exchange rate, and Keynes believed that the gap between British and American prices was greater than the government claimed, meaning that it was more serious. There was also a difference of opinion over how to interpret what had happened immediately after the war. WWI had been followed by a short-lived period in which wages had nearly doubled, and when this boom collapsed, wages had halved, returning to around their previous level. The authorities interpreted this as a sign that wages were flexible and could change easily. In contrast,

Keynes believed wages had fallen so rapidly only because people saw the previous year's rise as exceptional, and that under normal circumstances, reducing wages would be much more difficult, for workers would resist such a move. However, he had deeper objections to the policy: it was impossible to turn the clock back because the old order could never be restored. His arguments about monetary policy could be seen as further evidence for the claim, previously made in *Economic Consequences of the Peace*, that the Victorian era was not the period of stability it had been claimed to be.

His main analysis of the problem was published in a series of articles in the supplements he had edited for the *Manchester Guardian,* several of which were used as the basis for the book *A Tract on Monetary Reform* (1923). This began, not with technical economic analysis, but with a chapter on the social consequences of changes in the price level. Rising or falling prices had the effect of redistributing incomes between social groups: resources would be redistributed between debtors and creditors, and between wage-earners on fixed incomes. Inflation resulted in "*injustice* to those who in good faith have committed their savings to titles to money rather than to things."* Because it benefitted businesses, causing prices to rise in relation to costs, inflation stimulated economic activity, and deflation had the opposite effect. Changes in the value of money also had implications for public finance, a mechanism often referred to as the inflation tax. The details of these arguments, later admired even by Milton Friedman, are not important. What

---

* A Tract on Monetary Reform, The Collected Writings of John Maynard Keynes, vol IV (hereafter Tract), 29. Italics in original.

is important for the argument being made here is the conclusion Keynes drew.

> For these grave causes we must free ourselves from the deep distrust which exists against allowing the regulation of the standard of value [the price level] to be the subject of *deliberate decision*. We can no longer afford to leave it in the category of which the distinguishing characteristics are possessed in different degrees by the weather, the birth rate, and the Constitution—matters which are settled by natural causes, or are the resultant of the separate action of many individuals acting independently, or require a revolution to change them.*

He was taking the stance that changes in the price level had serious consequences and that policymakers should make deliberate decisions about what they wanted the price level to be. This relies on technical arguments about the consequences of price changes, but the heart of his position is a moral one: that the authorities should take responsibility for the price level.

Central to Keynes' analysis was the claim that exchange rate policy had direct consequences on the price level. Here, he drew on two well-established theories. One was the quantity theory of money, expounded by both his teacher, Marshall, and by Marshall's successor, Pigou. The other was the theory of purchasing power parity, recently used by the Swedish economist Gustav Cassel, to explain the dramatic exchange-rate fluctuations that had occurred during WWI. Essentially, the theory of purchasing power parity states

---

* Tract, 36. Italics in the original.

that internationally tradable goods must sell for the same price in different countries. Thus, if something costs £1 in Britain, and the exchange rate is £1 = $4.86, the item must sell for approximately $4.86 in the United States. The relationship will not be exact because of transport costs and other barriers to trade, but where these costs are low, it should be a good guide to what prices are appropriate.

Keynes concluded that the British authorities (the government and the Bank of England) had a choice. They could either conduct monetary policy to achieve a stable domestic price level or they could aim for a stable exchange rate. Given that they had no control over prices in the United States, they could not have both. In other words, they faced a choice between internal stability (stability of the domestic price level) and external stability (stability of the exchange rate).

This is where arguments about the social consequences of price changes came in. If, as was the case, the authorities stabilized the exchange rate, they had to accept whatever domestic price level was implied by purchasing power parity. Under the circumstances prevailing in the 1920s, that meant falling prices, downward pressure on wages, and stagnation, especially in industries dominated by export markets: textiles, iron and steel, coal mining, and shipbuilding. Such pressures led to social conflict as workers resisted wage cuts. Instead, Keynes argued it would be better to let policy be guided by domestic considerations, aiming for stable prices and accepting whatever exchange rate resulted, given circumstances in the rest of the world.

Keynes' argument developed into a full-blown attack on the gold standard. This went further than merely technical claims about whether the parity was or was not the correct one. He argued that the gold standard was based on a misconception about how policy should be conceived. The standard of value needed to be regulated—it was not a fact of nature—and the gold standard was a way of abdicating responsibility. Moreover, the arguments that were used to support the gold standard were already out of date.

> In truth, the gold standard is already a barbarous relic. All of us, from the Governor of the Bank of England downwards, are now primarily interested in preserving the stability of business, prices, and employment, and are not likely, when the choice is forced on us, deliberately to sacrifice these to the outworn dogma, which had its value once, of £3. 17s 10½d per ounce. Advocates of the ancient standard do not observe how remote it now is from the spirit and the requirements of the age. A regulated non-metallic standard has slipped in unnoticed. It *exists*. Whilst the economists dozed, the academic dream of a hundred years, doffing its cap and gown, clad in paper rags, has crept into the real world by means of the bad fairies—always so much more potent than the good—the wicked ministers of finance.*

His main message was that the government needed to take responsibility, an argument that was moral as much as economic.

In 1925, under Chancellor of the Exchequer Winston Churchill, now a Conservative, Britain returned to the gold standard. Keynes followed up his arguments with a critique of that decision in a series of articles in the *Evening Standard* newspaper. These were then expanded into a pamphlet published by the Hogarth Press, run by his Bloomsbury friends, Leonard and Virginia Woolf, titled "The Economic

* Tract, 138.

Consequences of Mr. Churchill" (1925). Like *A Tract on Monetary Reform*, this pamphlet showed the centrality of Keynes' journalism to his work in economics.

THE NEED TO COMBAT UNEMPLOYMENT

In another pamphlet published by the Hogarth Press in 1926, "The end of laissez faire," which was based on lectures given in Oxford and Berlin, Keynes reflected more generally on the problem of what the government should and should not do. Reviewing the history of the idea in the 18th and 19th centuries, Keynes argued that the doctrine of laissez-faire had arisen as a way of harmonizing the principles of individualism and socialism. Laissez-faire implied that egoism —pursuing one's own interest—led to the greatest good of the greatest number, the aim of socialism. For many years, Keynes argued, the doctrine seemed to be supported by the fact that the immense material progress that took place between the 1700s and 1800s owed more to private initiative than to public endeavors. However, although this was the view of many political philosophers, "economists of authority", such as John Stuart Mill, had been much more circumspect: though seeing much merit in the laissez-faire idea, they rarely rejected socialism altogether. In particular, Alfred Marshall had analyzed important cases where private and public interests were not the same. (Keynes could have added that Marshall's successor, Pigou, went even further in this direction.)

Keynes concluded it was impossible to settle the question of what role the state should play on purely abstract grounds. Private enterprise was important, but because private and public interests were not always the same, it was wrong to conclude that the state should do nothing. Adopting terminology taken from Jeremy Bentham, Keynes argued it was important to distinguish between the agenda and the non-agenda of the state and to derive a democratic system capable of achieving those things that the state needed to do. Of particular importance were those things which formed part of the state's agenda because, if the state did not do them, it would not do them at all. Here, he gave examples that reflected the problems with which he had the most experience. Uncertainty and ignorance turned big business into a lottery, creating inequalities in the distribution of wealth—fortunes for some and unemployment for others. Hence, control of credit and currency—monetary policy—needed to be undertaken by a central authority to avoid undesirable fluctuations in economic activity. He also argued that there needed to be some control over the volume of saving and investment, and the extent to which savings were invested abroad. In brief remarks that, in an age when eugenics was still fashionable in many quarters, were far less controversial than they would be today, Keynes noted that policy should cover the size of the population and that the time might be coming when attention should be paid to its innate quality as well as to its size. Keynes did not elaborate on these points, but they related to his long-standing interest in Malthus and in promoting birth control. In the early 20th century, there was widespread concern that, due to their use of contraception, the reduced fertility of the educated classes was lowering the overall intelligence of the population; Keynes held a relatively liberal position, arguing that, with growing prosperity and education, the poorer classes would adopt similar methods of birth control.

However, although Keynes was arguing about the role

the government should play, under a provocative title, he was no socialist. He believed in capitalism, concluding,

> For my part I think that capitalism, wisely managed, can probably be made more efficient for attaining economic ends than any alternative system yet in sight, but that in itself it is extremely objectionable. Our problem is to work out a social organisation which shall be as efficient as possible without offending our notions of a satisfactory way of life.*

The background to these remarks is that this was the time when the Soviet Union was being established, and many intellectuals were seduced by the prospects of what Sidney and Beatrice Webb described as "a new civilisation."† After his marriage to Lydia Lopokova, Keynes visited Russia and wrote about his experiences. He saw communism not as a new economic system but as a religion. Given the desire of many people to have something they could believe in, this could help account for the appeal of the new Soviet system, giving it an advantage over capitalism, which was completely irreligious. However, the religious dimension of communism held no appeal for him. Moreover, as a lifelong liberal, he saw freedom as a necessary part of a satisfactory life. He was therefore immune to the attractions of communism. His liberal convictions even stopped him from supporting the much milder socialism of the British Labour Party.

---

* Essays in Persuasion, The Collected Writings of John Maynard Keynes, vol. IX (hereafter EP), 294.

† Sidney and Beatrice Webb, Soviet Communism: A new civilisation.

Keynes' support for the Liberal Party is the background to his analysis of economic policy in the late 1920s. Until 1925, he opposed Britain's return to the gold standard because it would result in deflation and stagnation. Once this step had been taken, maintaining the parity required further deflation. Workers resisted the move, and their protests culminated in the General Strike of 1926. However, even if the cause of these problems was returning to gold at an inappropriate exchange rate, it was clear that the decision would not be reversed. Keynes, therefore, turned to alternative means of boosting employment: public works policy. Here he worked with colleagues in the Liberal Party, notably Hubert Henderson, helping organize a series of Liberal summer schools at which the party's policies were discussed.

Public works policy—building roads, schools, housing, and other public investment projects—had a long history as a way of reducing fluctuations in employment. The idea was that the authorities could identify necessary public works and earmark them to be undertaken when unemployment was high, thereby compensating for falls in private investment. Such policies were opposed by the Treasury, using the so-called "Treasury View." Articulated by Winston Churchill, this statement stated that spending on public projects merely displaced private spending: additional employment on public works would be matched by reduced employment in the private sector. Most economists, however, were skeptical of this argument. For example, when he succeeded Marshall in 1908, Pigou's inaugural lecture had been devoted to arguing against such a view.

The connection between Keynes' arguments on what we now call fiscal policy and the Liberal Party is made clear in a pamphlet he wrote, together with Henderson, in May 1929, as a contribution to the General Election campaign. The Liberal Party's election manifesto was *We can Conquer Unemployment*, with Lloyd George pledging to put in place public works projects that would reduce joblessness to normal levels within a year, raising no new taxes. Supporting this position in a pamphlet titled "Can Lloyd George Do It?", Keynes and Henderson argued that, although problems might arise in implementing the policy, it was basically sound and should be pursued. They explained that spending would be on useful schemes such as bringing the railways up to European standards and improving the housing stock so that even if the program ended up costing money, it would be well spent. But they claimed that the policy would pay for itself through increasing production and employment, attaching great importance to what they called "indirect employment." If a million pounds were spent employing men to build roads, there would be an increase in demand for raw materials and other goods, which would, in turn, create more jobs. And workers would receive wages that would be spent, further stimulating production. As for the charge that this was socialism, they argued it was already a fact that the rate of spending on capital projects depended on government policy. Echoing Keynes' argument in "The end of laissez-faire," they wrote, "it is a question of the state putting its hand to the job or of its not being done at all."*

As with the other works discussed in this chapter, Keynes' and Henderson's arguments were based on age-old economic ideas, but the two authors gave them a new twist

---

* EP, 113.

and combined them with thoughts about moral and political philosophy. As in those early works, he was using his literary skills to persuade his audience to embrace the future, rather than cling to the past.

> Negation, restriction, inactivity—these are the government's watchwords. Under their leadership we have been forced to button up our waistcoats and compress our lungs. Fears and doubts and hypochondriac precautions are keeping us muffled up indoors. But we are not tottering to our graves. We are healthy children. We need the breath of life. There is nothing to be afraid of. On the contrary. The future holds in store for us far more wealth and economic freedom and possibilities of personal life than the past has ever offered.
>
> There is no reason why we should not feel ourselves free to be bold, to be open, to experiment, to take action, to try the possibilities of things. And over against us, standing in the path, there is nothing but a few old gentlemen tightly buttoned-up in their frock coats, who only need to be treated with a little friendly disrespect and bowled over like ninepins.
>
> Quite likely they will enjoy it themselves, when once they have got over the shock.*

Like his Bloomsbury friends, Keynes wanted to move on from the past and into a new era.

---

* EP, 125.

3
WHY CAPITALISM SOMETIMES FAILS

THEORIES ABOUT THE GREAT DEPRESSION

Can Lloyd George Do It? was written against the background of the unemployment that Britain had experienced through most of the 1920s, a period when the United States had been booming—the so-called "Roaring Twenties." In October 1929, however, after the stock market crash, most of the world was plunged into a deep depression, and Britain, already suffering from stagnation, suffered even worse unemployment than in the 1920s. Depression created a massive hole in the public finances, to which the British government responded with further attempts to reduce public spending. Economists inevitably turned to analyzing the causes of this unprecedented crisis.

Keynes was drawn into the policy debates when, in November 1929, the government appointed a committee, chaired by Hugh Macmillan (not to be confused with either the future Prime Minister, Harold Macmillan, or Keynes' publisher, Daniel Macmillan) to inquire into the operation of banking, finance, and credit, and to make recommendations that might promote the development of trade, commerce, and employment. Though conceived before the stock market crash, this committee could not avoid considering the current situation, as well as longer-term problems facing British industry. Two months later, Keynes was also appointed to the Economic Advisory Council, a body chaired by the Prime Minister, Ramsay MacDonald, that would provide economic advice to the government. Together, these committees demanded much of Keynes' time, the Macmillan committee's report not appearing until 1931, after the Committee had interviewed a long series of witnesses. The work involved reading memoranda submitted in advance and then cross-examining witnesses about their evidence. Keynes was also heavily involved in the report's writing.

At one level, this was ideal timing, for Keynes had been thinking seriously about monetary economics for years, and these committees gave him a platform from which to influence policy. On another level, however, the timing was unfortunate because, by November 1929, he was in the middle of finishing a two-volume work on monetary economics—*A Treatise on Money* (1930)—and his committee work meant that he was under enormous time-pressure. To understand the significance of this project, it is necessary to note that by this point, Keynes had a reputation as one of the world's leading monetary economists, but he had not published a major study on the subject. He had written much, but his most influential books, *Economic Consequences of the Peace* and *A Tract on Monetary Reform*, were far from being academic treatises; they were responses to immediate policy issues, drawing on theories that were well known and initially aimed at a wide audience. As such, they provided flimsy foundations for a secure academic reputation. This was to be provided by the new book. The first volume covered the pure theory of money, and the second, the applied theory.

The *Treatise on Money* marked a move away from the Marshallian quantity theory that had provided the basis for his analysis of monetary problems in the 1920s. An important characteristic of his theory was that it explained the changes in the price level not in terms of the money supply (the approach of the quantity theory) but in terms of the gap between saving and investment. Separating saving and investment in this way was more challenging than it would be today because economists widely assumed that, except temporarily, savings would automatically be invested in productive assets, because it was thought irrational to save money merely to hoard it. The result was that saving and investment were widely treated as synonymous: even the terminology for discussing the two concepts was not agreed upon. This was a problem on which Keynes had worked closely with a Cambridge colleague, Dennis Robertson, assisting him with his book *Banking Policy and the Price Level* (1926). Robertson had distinguished between saving (abstinence from consumption) and investment (the purchase of productive assets), along with making many further distinctions relating to the motives for saving and investment. Keynes did not adopt Robertson's extremely elaborate and confusing terminology, but he followed Robertson in distinguishing between saving and investment. Saving and investment could differ, he argued, because that investment might be funded either by saving or by what he called "windfall profits"—revenue that would arise when firms received a higher price for their product than they had anticipated.

This was the basis for a theory that explained how monetary policy could affect the level of output. Monetary policy, operating through the financial system, determined the interest rate, and this determined the gap between saving and investment. Low interest rates would deter saving, but they would encourage investment. If investment were higher than saving, prices would rise, resulting in windfall profits; high profits, in turn, would encourage firms to increase production, thereby employing more labor and reducing unemployment. In contrast, high interest rates would have the opposite effect. The result was a theory about how monetary policy, under the restored Gold Standard, with a fixed exchange rate, could regulate the level of economic activity. It was a hypothesis that echoed the theory developed by the Swedish economist, Knut Wicksell, at the end of the 19th century.

This was the context for Keynes' only public debate with the Austrian economist Friedrich Hayek. In 1930-31, Hayek had been invited to the London School of Economics to give a series of lectures on his new theory of the business cycle. When Keynes' *Treatise on Money* appeared, Hayek wrote a very substantial technical review in the LSE journal, *Economica*. Keynes and Hayek were both analyzing the depression using a theory centered on the relationship between saving and investment that could be traced back to Wicksell. However, they reached opposing conclusions about the appropriate policy response. Keynes argued that low interest rates were required to stimulate investment, which would raise output and employment. Against this,

Hayek argued that excessively low interest rates had caused the boom in the 1920s, and that to fight unemployment in this way was to throw oil on the fire. Hayek's remedy was to end the loose monetary policy that he considered the cause of the crisis and to accept that a temporary rise in unemployment was inevitable.

Hayek's main target was Keynes' theory of production—his account of the relationship between interest rates, capital, and production. While the theory of capital played a major role in Hayek's own theory of the depression, Keynes believed it was irrelevant to his own hypothesis. Typically, for a 30-year-old taking on the ideas of an establishment figure two decades his senior, Hayek pulled no punches in his critique of Keynes' theory, and when Hayek's book appeared, Keynes, in his reply to Hayek, reciprocated with equally blunt criticisms. Each found the other's arguments incomprehensible. The following year, Hayek produced the second installment of his review, but this time, to Hayek's great frustration, Keynes did not respond, simply explaining that his thinking had now moved on.

The reason Keynes had changed his mind was that he had received criticisms from a group of young economists in Cambridge, who had met to discuss the book in an informal seminar that came to be known as "the Circus." These economists—including Piero Sraffa, Joan and Austin Robinson, James Meade, and Richard Kahn—discussed the book, with Kahn playing the role of "the messenger angel" who brought messages and problems from Keynes to the Circus and, in the words of one of its members, "went back to heaven with the results of our deliberations." They found*

* D. E. Moggridge, Maynard Keynes: An Economist's Biography, 530-1.

fault with what Keynes had called his "fundamental equations," on which his policy conclusions rested. The crucial point was one Ralph Hawtrey had made earlier. He was a former member of the Apostles, author of one of the leading textbooks on money (*Currency and Credit,* 1919), and now an economist at the Treasury, to whom Keynes had sent page proofs. Hawtrey claimed Keynes had made a serious logical error in claiming that an excess of investment over saving caused prices to rise because he had defined investment and saving in such a way that investment would automatically exceed saving if prices had risen. The fundamental equations were a tautology—they were true because that was the way variables had been defined—and so they could explain nothing. There was a further problem in that Keynes was also trying to analyze changes in output with a theory that took output as a given. Hawtrey had made these points before the book was published, but Keynes had been so busy with his work on the Macmillan Committee that he had been unable to digest them properly.

Keynes had never been completely happy with his book. When he finished it, he told his mother, "Artistically it is a failure—I have changed my mind too much in the course of it for it to be a proper unity."* His first reaction to criticisms was that he needed to present the argument differently, but he rapidly concluded that a more radical change of approach was needed. He, therefore, started work on a new book, a task that would take several years. This time, instead of working on it alone, he discussed it thoroughly with his Cambridge colleagues in the Circus.

Kahn, whose undergraduate work Keynes had recently

* ibid, pp. 530-1.

supervised, was important in another way for the development of Keynes' theory. Keynes set him the task of working out how many additional men would be employed as a result of hiring an additional person on a public works program (it was normal to speak of men in those days, even if some jobs would be taken by women). In other words, he wanted Kahn to quantify the "indirect employment" that had been so important in *Can Lloyd George Do It?* Kahn came up with the solution known as the "multiplier." When an additional man is employed, k more men will have to be employed to produce the additional goods that will be demanded. The number k will depend on how much of his wages the worker spends and how much is spent out of any profits earned by his employer, and will clearly be less than one, because some income will be saved and some income is likely to be spent on imported goods. Those k men will, in turn, create secondary employment for k^2 men. These k^2 men will then generate secondary employment for k^3 men, and so on. This is an infinite series, but because k is less than one, the terms are getting smaller and smaller until they become vanishingly minute. Simple mathematics shows that it adds up to a definite amount and that the total employment created, including the man employed on the public works project, is $1/(1\text{-}k)$ men. Thus, if $k$was about ½, as Keynes believed, then the total employment resulting from employing one more man would be 2 men (1 + ½ + ¼ + ⅛ + ...). If k were ⅔, then the total would be 3 men, and so on. Clearly, to derive this result, Kahn had to make enormous simplifying assumptions, such as that the wage rate did not change and the average cost of output did not rise as employment increased, but it provided a framework within which the problem could be analyzed. For example, if there were little spare capacity in the economy, then increases in spending would raise prices, reducing the rise in employment.

Over the next few years, Keynes worked on his new book, presenting successive versions of his thinking in the lecture course he gave each year in Cambridge, as well as in guest lectures given at other places. Of particular importance in illustrating the progress of was a series of articles in *The Times* newspaper, which Keynes expanded into a pamphlet published as *The Means to Prosperity* (1933). The significance of this work is that instead of arguing, as he had done in the *Treatise*, that increases in output are caused by rising profit margins, here he adopted Kahn's theory of the multiplier, according to which changes in demand affect output directly. This is the mechanism to which Keynes had been blind when Ohlin had used it in debating reparations payments. However, rather than dwell on the stages by which Keynes reached his new theory, which would take us into technical details, we turn directly to the book.

SAVING AND THE MULTIPLIER

The General Theory of Employment, Interest and Money was published in February 1936. The most important feature of the book is that it is not concerned with economic policy, but is a work of economic theory addressed to his fellow economists. He stated this very clearly in the opening line of the Preface. His goal was to explain why periods of mass unemployment were possible—why capitalism could sometimes fail. Although it had important policy implications, it was not a recipe for action but, rather, a theoretical question about how the world worked and how it should be analyzed.

Keynes began the book with a critique of what he called the "classical" theory. The term "classical" was a familiar one, having been used in the middle of the 19th century by Karl Marx to refer to the work of his predecessors, but Keynes' usage was different and unfamiliar. He applied it to the economists who believed in what he called Say's Law. This was the doctrine positing that when the economy is considered as a whole, there can never be a shortage of demand for goods and services because supply creates its own demand. To understand what this means, suppose that a business, or group of businesses, decides to increase its production of certain goods. They are augmenting the supply of goods and also generating incomes, because they are paying more wages to their workers and they are earning more profits that increase the wealth of their shareholders. Say's Law states that these incomes are exactly sufficient to buy the quantity of goods produced: producing $100 worth of goods generates incomes of $100. (If the firm buys raw materials or components, then the same analysis can be applied to the firms that supply the raw materials and components and, in turn, to the firms that supply the suppliers.) It is, of course, possible that the wrong goods are being produced. If producers decide to manufacture more shoes when people want to buy more overcoats, there will be a glut of shoes and a shortage of overcoats. But when you add together the values of all goods produced, there is a balance: the glut of shoes must exactly cancel out the shortage of overcoats. There can be no scarcity of aggregate demand. The result was that, instead of being used to refer simply to Marx's predecessors, Keynes was using the term "classical economics" as a label for a line of thought that ran all the way from Jean-Baptiste Say and his contemporary, David Ricardo, writing in the early 1800s, to Keynes' own contemporaries writing in the 1930s.

The doctrine that supply creates its own demand is the same as the claim that saving and investment will always be equal (this follows from the way saving and investment are defined). The "classical" explanation of this equality (and I put quotation marks around the term "classical" as a reminder that this was Keynes' new and unfamiliar terminology) was that savings would not be hoarded—that is, people would not just store banknotes under the mattress—because that was irrational. Why should anyone do that if they could earn interest by investing or lending the money to people who wanted to use it productively? They would either use savings to finance their own business activities or, more likely, deposit their savings in a bank or other financial institution, and the bank would then lend it to someone who wanted to undertake an investment. Savings would, therefore, get channeled into investment. The mechanism that would ensure a balance between saving and investment was the rate of interest: if businesses did not want to invest as much as households were saving, the rate of interest would fall, reducing households' incentive to save and making it more attractive for businesses to invest. In the terminology used at the time, the rate of interest equated to supply and demand for loanable funds.

Keynes set himself the task of showing that this doctrine was mistaken by constructing an alternative theory of what determined the level of output or income (the two terms can be treated as synonymous). In this theory, equilibrium is brought about not by price changes but by changes in output, which are directly linked to changes in aggregate demand. The easiest way to see how this can happen is to make a distinction that Keynes failed to make clear in the *General Theory*, between planned investment—the volume of investment that businesses want to undertake given the circumstances in which they find themselves—and actual investment. These can be different because, if firms fail to sell the quantity of goods they expected to sell, they will find that their inventories—their stocks of unsold goods—will be higher than anticipated. This will be recorded in the national accounts as investment in inventories. The mechanism linking saving and investment to changes in output is that, if saving exceeds planned investment, there will be a shortfall in aggregate demand, and inventories will accumulate; this will be a signal that businesses should reduce their production. In contrast, if saving is less than planned investment, inventories will be run down, signaling to firms that they should increase production. Equilibrium is where saving and planned investment are equal. The level of production determines the level of employment.

A crucial part of this theory is what Keynes called the consumption function, because this explains the fraction of income spent on consumption goods and hence the fraction that is saved. After listing a range of factors on which consumption depends, Keynes argued that while unexpected changes in the value of households' capital assets, large changes in the interest rate, or fiscal policy might change consumption behavior, there would typically be a stable relationship between consumption and income.

> The fundamental psychological law, upon which we are entitled to depend with great confidence both *a priori* from

> our knowledge of human nature and from the detailed facts of experience, is that men are disposed, as a rule and on the average, to increase their consumption as their income increases, but not by as much as the amount of the increase in their income.*

In other words, Keynes was saying that because saving is defined as whatever households do not consume, as incomes rise, people save a higher fraction of that increased revenue.

A key variable is what Keynes called "the marginal propensity to consume." This is the fraction of any increase in income that will be consumed. If it is 3⁄4, that means that if earnings rise (or fall) by $100, consumption will also rise (or fall) by $75. Though expressed in terms of incomes, not employment, it is essentially the same variable as the *k* that appeared in Kahn's multiplier, discussed earlier. It means that if investment changes by $100, it will cause consumption to rise by the multiplier times $100. In our example, that means that total output (consumption plus investment) will rise by 4 x $100 = $400. Therefore, in Keynes' theory, the given level of investment can explain what the level of income will be.

FINANCE AND INVESTMENT

To complete this theory, Keynes also needed a hypothesis about investment. Investment refers to spending on productive assets: it takes place when a business buys buildings,

---

* The General Theory of Employment, Interest and Money, The Collected Writings of John Maynard Keynes, vol.VII (hereafter GT), 96.

vehicles, machinery, or stocks of raw materials and components that it will use to provide goods and services, or when a business decides to hold stocks of finished goods ready for sale. This depends on factors that differ greatly from those affecting the consumption-saving decision. Investment will take place only if firms expect it to be profitable, and that will depend on what the investment costs, on how much output it will produce, and the prices that firms expect to get for that output. The main problem, both for the businesses and for the economist analyzing investment, is that the future is unknown. We may have a good idea of what will happen in the next few months or even the next year or so, but beyond that, Keynes argued, we know very little. As he put it in one of the most remarkable chapters of his book,

> The outstanding fact is the extreme precariousness of the basis of knowledge on which our estimates of prospective yield [the profitability of a new factory or other long-lived investment] have to be made. Our knowledge of the factors which will govern the yield of an investment some years hence is usually very slight and often negligible. If we speak frankly, we have to admit that our basis of knowledge for estimating the yield ten years hence of a railway, copper mine, a textile factory, the goodwill of a patent medicine, an Atlantic liner, a building in the City of London amounts to little and sometimes to nothing; or even five years hence.*

Yet managers and those who are providing them with funds have to make such decisions all the time. How do they

* GT, 149-50.

do this? Keynes, drawing on years of experience in the City of London, and also as a fund manager, argued that people fall back on conventions: they assume that the future will be much like the present. As long as the convention holds, all will be well. However, conventional valuations formed in this way are very precarious. The value of a company depends not so much on what it is "really" worth as on what investors think it is worth. Everyone is trying to second-guess everyone else. Investment is therefore not a matter of rational calculation but is subject to the whims of mass psychology, liable to change at a moment's notice.

The crucial point here is that saving and investment are determined by completely different factors: saving depends on what households have consumed, which, in turn, is based primarily on their incomes. Investment, on the other hand, depends on expectations of the future and the psychology of markets. What of the rate of interest? Why can this not work to bring about a balance? If investment were a matter of rational calculation, perhaps it could; but the role played by spontaneous optimism or pessimism—fluctuations in "animal spirits," as Keynes called them—makes this difficult. And there is yet another problem.

Keynes argued that the rate of interest was not determined by saving and investment (productivity and thrift) but by what he called "liquidity preference." When people save, they accumulate wealth, and this wealth needs to be held in some sort of asset. Liquidity is the ability to turn assets into something that can be spent. Cash is obviously the most liquid asset, followed by bank deposits and other short-term financial assets (for example, for a corporation, US Treasury Bills, which mature in less than 90 days, are highly liquid as their price will not change much and they are easy to sell). Long-term bonds or equities are less liquid because, although they are easy to turn into cash, the price at which they can be sold is liable to fluctuate, making their value uncertain. Physical assets, such as a home, a factory, or a piece of industrial machinery, are even less liquid. Keynes' point was that the rate of interest determines whether it is worthwhile to invest in illiquid assets instead of having the security of holding their wealth as money. The rate of interest will adjust to make the amount of money people want to hold equal to the supply.

Add to this the assumption that when there is unemployment and factories are lying idle, as during the Great Depression, production and employment are determined by aggregate demand, not by limits to productive capacity, and you have a theory that runs as follows: given the level of liquidity preference, which determines the demand for money, changes in the money supply (monetary policy) determine the rate of interest. The rate of interest, together with businesses' expectations about the future, determines the level of investment. Investment then determines consumption, income, and employment, via the multiplier.

A MORE GENERAL THEORY

Throughout this argument, Keynes was ignoring the mechanism that many of his contemporaries believed would bring about full employment. High unemployment should lead to cuts in wages, which will induce businesses to employ more labor. It may be true that if an individual worker offers to work for a lower wage, potential employers may hire him or her in preference to a worker who is being paid more (though there are many reasons for doubting that real-world labor markets work like this). And if all the workers in a particular business accept a cut in wages, the company will have lower costs and will be able to reduce its prices, taking business away from other producers. However—and this is the crucial point—if all workers in the nation as a whole take a wage cut, the consequences will be different: production costs and hence prices may fall, but so too will the incomes available to purchase goods and services. The crucial question is whether lower wage rates cause a rise or a fall in aggregate demand.

Keynes approached this problem by listing seven ways in which a decrease in wage rates and the resulting drop in prices could affect aggregate demand.

> (1) It will redistribute income in favor of people on fixed incomes (as he had explained in *The Tract on Monetary Reform*). As those on fixed incomes were generally wealthier, saving a higher fraction of their income, this was likely to reduce aggregate demand.
>
> (2) It would reduce domestic wages compared foreign wages, making domestic producers more competitive in relation to foreign producers. This would increase aggregate demand.
>
> (3) It would reduce living standards through diminished incomes relative to the price of imported goods. This would reduce aggregate demand.
>
> (4) If the wage cut was believed to be temporary, or if it were believed to be a sign of further cuts in future, firms might have an incentive to change their investment. The prospect of lower costs might make investment more attractive, but companies might decide to postpone

> investment until wages were even lower. The effect could go either way.
>
> (5) Falling incomes would reduce the demand for cash, tending to lower the interest rate, stimulating investment and aggregate demand.
>
> (6) Wage cuts might make businessmen more optimistic, or they might lead to labor unrest. This effect could go either way.
>
> (7) Falling prices will increase the burden of firms' debts, perhaps causing some to go bankrupt. This could reduce investment and aggregate demand.

Keynes' conclusion was that, overall, the effect of wage cuts could go either way and therefore such reductions were not reliable in achieving full employment. Indeed, the opposite was true: stability of prices and wages might reduce uncertainty, thereby increasing investment and aggregate demand.

As Keynes had explained at the start of the book, it was a work of economic theory, addressed to his fellow economists. It was also a long book, containing many technical arguments, not all of which have been discussed here. However, because of Keynes' celebrity status, the book was eagerly awaited, and Keynes, whose contract with his publisher enabled him to set the price, valued it very low, at five shillings ($1.25 at the prevailing exchange rates), which was much less than books of this type usually sold for. In the United States, it costs two dollars. Sales were high, and the book was widely reviewed in newspapers and general magazines that would not normally carry reviews of economics books. Random examples from the hundred-plus English-language reviews to appear by the end of 1936 illustrate this: *Liverpool Post, The Scotsman, Servant of India, Christchurch Star Sun, Brisbane Telegraph, New York Herald Tribune, Springfield Republican, Edmonton Journal,* and *Toronto Star.*

In the book's final chapter, titled "Concluding notes on the social philosophy towards which the general theory might lead,"[5] Keynes took up an argument that he had made in *Economic Consequences of the Peace.* He challenged the notion that high volumes of savings necessarily led to capital accumulation and prosperity. High savings, the *General Theory* had shown, could simply lead to stagnation and unemployment. This removed a major justification for a very unequal distribution of income and undermined the widely held view that inheritance taxes were responsible for reducing the country's capital stock. Keynes believed that inequality had gone too far: "It is not necessary for the stimulation of these activities and the satisfaction of these proclivities that the game should be played for such high stakes as at present. Much lower stakes will serve the purpose equally well, as soon as the players are accustomed to them." There was therefore scope for making the distribution of income more equal. However, Keynes was not egalitarian in that he believed there was justification for considerable inequalities of wealth. There were valuable activities that would not take place without the incentive of making money, and money-making provided comparatively harmless channels into which "dangerous human proclivities" could be diverted. "It is better," he wrote, "that a man should tyrannise over his bank balance than over his fellow-citizens."*

* GT, 374.

Keynes then proceeded to an argument that many reviewers were to take up, concerning what he called "the euthanasia of the rentier."* High interest rates had often been justified by the need to stimulate saving. In contrast, his theory suggested that prosperity—full employment—might require low interest rates. Moreover, if full employment could be sustained, it might be possible to create so much capital that it would no longer be scarce. If this could be achieved, the rate of interest might fall to a very low level, reducing the returns on investment, as well as "the capitalist class' oppressive power to exploit the scarcity value of capital."† He concluded:

> I see, therefore, the rentier aspect of capitalism as a transitional phase that will disappear when it has done its work. And with the disappearance of its rentier aspect much else in it besides will suffer a sea-change. It will be, moreover, a great advantage of the order of events which I am advocating, that the euthanasia of the rentier, of the functionless investor, will be nothing sudden, merely a gradual but prolonged continuance of what we have seen recently in Great Britain, and will need no revolution.

Such a change did not mean the end of individualism because, as Keynes had argued much earlier, the role of the state would be confined to determining the level of investment, not its composition. Despite writing provocatively about "the socialisation of investment," he was not advo-

* GT, 376.
† GT, 376.

cating state socialism, for he immediately went on to write about the merits of individualism.

> Let us stop for a moment to remind ourselves what these advantages [of individualism] are. They are partly advantages of efficiency—the advantages of decentralisation and the play of self interest. The advantage to efficiency of the decentralisation of decisions and of individual responsibility is even greater, perhaps, than the nineteenth century supposed; and the reaction against the appeal to self-interest may have gone too far. But, above all, individualism, if it can be purged of its defects and its abuses, is the best safeguard of personal liberty in the sense that, compared with any other system, it greatly widens the field for the exercise of personal choice. It is also the best safeguard of the variety of life, which emerges precisely from this extended field of personal choice, and the loss of which is the greatest of all the losses of the homogeneous or totalitarian state.*

He favored government intervention to cure unemployment, but not government control of economic activity in general. The implications of the *General Theory*, Keynes believed, were "moderately conservative."†

Was there, Keynes asked, any hope that a work of economic theory could change the world? He believed that, given the circumstances of the time, people were open to a fundamental diagnosis of the problem—an analysis that got to the heart of the main problem facing society, and he

* GT, 380.

† GT, 377.

expressed hope that his book could eventually lead to change.

> [T]he ideas of economists and political philosophers, both when they are right and when they are wrong, are more powerful than is commonly understood. Indeed, the world is ruled by little else. Practical men, who believe themselves to be quite exerts from any intellectual influences, are usually the slaves of some defunct economist. Madmen in authority, who hear voices in the air, are distilling their frenzy from some academic scribbler of a few years back. I am sure the power of vested interests is vastly exaggerated compared with the gradual encroachment of ideas. Not, indeed, immediately, but after a certain interval.*

In a letter to his friend, the playwright George Bernard Shaw, Keynes was more specific, telling him he was writing a book that he believed would transform the way the world thought about economic problems over the next 10 years.

This takes us to the next stage in the story of Keynesian economics, when others took over his ideas: the changes that came to be called the Keynesian revolution. Keynes remained active, especially in policy-making, for another decade, but the story of Keynesian economics ceases to be the story of Keynes himself, becoming the story of a much wider group of economists.

---

* GT, 383.

4
CHANGING THE WAY THE WORLD THINKS

CONVERTING OTHER ECONOMISTS

Keynes' book was eagerly awaited. As an example of the younger generation's enthusiasm, a group of Harvard economists arranged to have copies shipped over from Britain before it was published in the United States. Discussions of the book and its ideas rapidly eclipsed other debates about unemployment and the business cycle, of which there were many. To understand the reaction to the book, it is important to note several points.

The most important point is that, although the theory had clear implications for policy, it was a work of economic theory. Except for the very speculative final chapter, nothing was mentioned about economic policy. Furthermore, although the *General Theory* was not a mathematical book by the standards of modern economics (it contained some algebra and a single diagram), much of Keynes' verbal reasoning was couched in mathematical language—the language of functions, schedules, and curves. This meant that non-economists who read it had to grapple with a theory they found difficult. The result was that many reviewers, and no doubt many readers as well, focused on the final chapter, the one they found easiest to understand. As its title indicated, this chapter did not deal with the details of policies that needed to be implemented in the 1930s, but speculated on more fundamental implications of the theory.

Economists found the book difficult for different reasons. Following the example of Einstein, whose theory of relativity was more general than Isaac Newton's, Keynes presented his theory as more general than the classical version. The problem, he argued, was not the classical logic, but that the assumptions on which the classical theory was based were rarely satisfied in practice. However, if state action could maintain full employment, the classical theory, which assumes full employment, would "come into its own."* This might sound simple, but it was not.

One complication was that, as mentioned earlier, Keynes used the term "classical" economics in an unfamiliar way. The result was that many economists did not recognize their own ideas in what they considered a caricature of their views. Pigou, who had been picked out for criticism in the book, responded by stating:

> Einstein actually did for Physics what Mr. Keynes believes himself to have done for Economics. He developed a far-reaching generalization, under which Newton's results can be subsumed as a special case. But he did not, in announcing his discovery, insinuate, through carefully

---

* GT, 378.

barbed sentences, that Newton and those who had followed his lead were a gang of incompetent bunglers.*

Pigou had a reason for reacting this way because, aside from the issue of whether Keynes' sarcasm was justified, he had been on Keynes' side in many debates over policy. He supported public works policy and was skeptical about the ability of wage cuts to increase employment. Part of the problem was that, where Keynes saw a uniform "traditional" theory, many economists perceived immense variety and resisted his attempt to force them into a single box. Such variety was hardly surprising, given that research into business cycles had proliferated during the 20th century. Keynes' statement about how the classical theory might come into its own if government took action to ensure full employment raised further issues about the generality of his new theory and the extent of his break with orthodoxy. The debates that followed the publication of the *General Theory* focused as much on what the classical theory was as on Keynes' new theory.

A further important point about the book concerns Keynes' use of mathematics. His verbal arguments were framed around ideas that could be expressed in algebra, but went beyond what could be stated in algebra. Nowhere is this clearer than in the theory of consumption. The core of the theory is a relationship between consumption and income that takes the form $C = a + bY$, where C is aggregate consumption, Y is income, a is the level of consumption that would occur if income were zero, and b is the marginal propensity to consume. Yet if we read the verbal account of

---

* Pigou, Economica 1936, 115.

consumption in the *General Theory*, we find Keynes discussing the effect of asset values on consumption, the impact of interest rate changes, and psychological factors that affect consumption. Similarly with investment and the rate of interest: as explained in the previous chapter, he provided an account of investment that drew heavily on his own experience of market psychology, and he paid great attention to the role of expectations in determining the demand for money and interest rates. However, the algebra simply gave investment as a function of the rate of interest, ignoring psychological factors to which Keynes clearly attached great importance.

As a result, it is possible to extract a small mathematical model from the *General Theory*. It comprises a consumption function, an investment function relating investment to the rate of interest, and a demand for money function in which demand for money depends on income and the rate of interest (if income rises, people will want to hold more money; if the rate of interest rises, they will want to hold less). These three functions can be put together into a simple mathematical model that can be solved for output and the rate of interest as a function of the variables that are taken as given. This is what mathematically inclined economists started to do immediately after Keynes' book appeared. The most influential one of these was produced by the British economist John Hicks; it summed up the model with a diagram containing two curves. The point where they crossed indicated the equilibrium level of income and the rate of interest. It was then possible to analyze the effects of policy interventions by shifting the curves up and down to see how the equilibrium point changed. The difference between Keynesian and classical results can be shown by making different assumptions about the shapes of the two curves. Different assumptions about the slopes of the curves will lead to different predictions about the effect of policy changes, explaining why classical and Keynesian theories produced different outcomes. Though Hicks presented his model in September 1936, it is almost universally known as the IS-LM model—the labels for the two curves in the account that the American economist, Alvin Hansen, used in his *A Guide to Keynes* (1953). Note that, of the seven possible effects of wage cuts mentioned in the *General Theory*, only one, the effect on the money market and the rate of interest (number 5 in the list in Chapter 3), is present in the IS-LM model. That helps to explain why most economists reached different conclusions from Keynes on the significance of wage flexibility.

The 1930s were a time when a significant number of economists were turning to mathematical economics, using both algebra to develop economic theories and formal statistical methods to analyze economic data. It is no coincidence that Hicks' model was presented at a conference organized by the Econometric Society, the organization formed in 1930 to promote mathematical economics. Mathematical modeling made it possible to check the consistency of Keynes' analysis—whether his assumptions did indeed lead to the conclusions that he claimed they did—and in this sense, it was very useful. But it also led economists to neglect, or at least downplay, those ideas that did not fit into the mathematics, raising questions about whether mathematical models were faithful to Keynes' ideas.

A further problem was that the book contained many lines of argument. The Cambridge economist, Joan Robinson, who had been a member of the "Circus" and who became an important interpreter of Keynes, later claimed that the *General Theory* contained many lines of argument, some of which led nowhere and were not needed for the main point. Keynes should have erased all the incomplete lines of argument that did not lead anywhere, she posited, because they made it harder to see the argument that he had completed. There was thus ample scope for critics to pick up on details that Keynes thought were incidental to his main point.

The result of this lack of clarity about the main point Keynes was making is that when Keynes was invited in 1937 by the editor of Harvard's *Quarterly Journal of Economics* to respond to a group of eminent economists who had each written a substantial review of his book, he decided not to address their criticisms in detail, focusing instead on what he considered to be the main point that they had overlooked.

This central point, Keynes argued, was that the classical system dealt with a system in which resources were given and relevant facts were known. Expectations concerning the future and the risks people faced were assumed to be capable of "an exact actuarial computation."* In contrast, Keynes wrote,

> we have, as a rule, only the vaguest idea of any but the most direct consequences of our acts. ... The whole object of the accumulation of Wealth is to produce results, or potential results, at a comparatively distant date, and

---

* Keynes, "The General Theory of Employment", Quarterly Journal of Economics, in The Collected Writings of John Maynard Keynes, vol. XIV (hereafter QJE), 213

> sometimes at an *indefinitely* distant, date. The fact that our knowledge of the future is fluctuating, vague and uncertain, renders Wealth a peculiarly unsuitable subject for the methods of the classical economic theory. ... By "uncertain" knowledge, let me explain, I do not mean merely to distinguish what is known for certain from what is only probable. The game of roulette is not subject, in this sense, to uncertainty; nor is the prospect of a Victory bond being drawn. ... The sense in which I am using the term is that in which the prospect of a European war is uncertain, or the price of copper and the rate of interest twenty years hence, or the obsolescence of a new invention, of the position of private wealth-owners in the social system in 1970. About these matters, there is no scientific basis on which to form any calculable probability whatever. We simply do not know.*

This left open the question of how economists should analyze such situations. Keynes fell back on social psychology, drawing on his experience of business and financial markets, but other economists adopted different strategies.

Inevitably, when economists tried to make sense of Keynes' ideas, they related them to their own thinking. An excellent and highly influential example of this was Alvin Hansen, a Harvard economist who ended up being a major proponent of Keynesian economics in the United States. Hansen was a business cycle theorist who developed a theory relating investment to long-term, structural factors in the American economy. He saw population growth and innovation—new industries such as railroads, electric

---

* QJE, 213-14.

power, and the automobile—as major drivers of investment; in contrast to Keynes, whose theory was static, Hansen focused on how the economic system changed. This led him to concentrate on the possibility of long-term stagnation—so-called secular stagnation caused by falling population growth and a slowdown in the pace of innovation. This explained investment (in a way very different from Keynes' interpretation), but to complete his theory, he needed a theory of consumption. Hansen recognized that Keynes' multiplier provided what he needed, and so he incorporated it into his own theory. The result was that Hansen created a more dynamic theory of the business cycle than Keynes had provided, conceiving investment differently from Keynes, but using the multiplier in a way that made the theory seem Keynesian. He focused on the business cycle rather than just on what determined output and employment at a point in time. Another way of viewing Hansen's theory is to say that he reinterpreted Keynesian theory to fit what he believed were the distinctive features of the US economy.

Hansen was important in his own right, but also because he exerted a profound influence on Paul Samuelson, a Harvard graduate student. In 1939, Samuelson created a mathematical representation of Hansen's theory of the business cycle that incorporated Keynes' theory of the multiplier: the so-called multiplier-accelerator model. The acceleration principle, which was widely used by Hansen and many other American business cycle theorists, assumed businesses needed more capital in order to produce higher output; as a result, investment, which relates to the increase in the capital stock, must be related to the *increase* in output. The multiplier was a relationship between investment and the *level* of output. When the two were put together, the result was a dynamic theory explaining how output would change over time. The Keynesian element in this theory was a drastically simplified version of his theory, omitting complications such as the money market, liquidity preference, and the effect of interest rate changes on investment. Samuelson's theory was Keynesian in that it used the multiplier to explain the level of output, but it drew on Hansen and interwar American business cycle theory, not on Keynes, for its explanation of investment.

WINNING THE SECOND WORLD WAR

Hansen and an economist at the Federal Reserve, Lauchlin Currie, were important figures in bringing Keynesian ideas to the attention of the American government. A body called the Temporary National Economic Committee, involving members of both the US Senate and the House of Representatives, was conducting a massive inquiry into the concentration of economic power in the United States. Its scale is indicated by the fact that it produced around 30 volumes of reports supported by a further 30 volumes of evidence. The motivation for this inquiry was a belief that the Great Depression had occurred because the competitive mechanism had broken down due to the rise of monopoly—an accumulation of economic power. The committee's focus had been on whether the markets for goods and services were no longer sufficiently competitive to allow for the creativity and change considered essential to the prosperity of the American economy. Hansen and Currie shifted the committee's attention to what they called "the financial machine"—the mechanism whereby the financial system translated savings into investment. They argued that it was the financial machine that had broken down. Even though they chose not to mention Keynes (a story was circulating that there was a list of words that were taboo on the grounds that they would immediately alienate members of Congress, and that "Keynes" was one of these words), this was precisely the mechanism that Keynes was discussing in the *General Theory*: his main point was that there was no mechanism for ensuring that the volume of investment would be the same as the amount to save at full employment. However, by the time Hansen and Currie testified before the Committee in 1939, recovery was underway, and concerns were shifting to the impending war, planning for which began long before the United States became involved.

The *General Theory* was written against the background of the Great Depression, when prices were falling, unemployment was high, and there was massive excess capacity. However, the Keynesian concept of aggregate demand was to prove extremely useful when conditions changed, with an acute shortage of resources and the danger of inflation at the forefront. An early step towards applying the theory in wartime was taken by Keynes himself in a short book, *How to Pay for the War*, published in February 1940. Typically for Keynes, who was now back in the Treasury, this was an expansion of two articles published in *The Times* the previous November, a little over two months after the war had broken out in Europe.

The crucial background to what happened to Keynesian economics during the war was the development of national income accounting. There had long been estimates of national income, but these had typically been produced by individuals. For example, as early as the 17th century, estimates of English national income had been calculated by estimating the incomes of the different classes of society, multiplying those by the number of people believed to be in each social class, and adding up the total level of income. (The purpose of that calculation had been to estimate how long England would be able to afford to carry on its war with the Netherlands.) The problem was that the systematic collection of the data was a task beyond the resources of any private organization, let alone a single economist working alone. For example, company accounts might provide some data required on business activity, but getting the systematic data required for the construction of reliable national accounts requires that the government collect the statistics, forcing businesses to provide these figures in the necessary format. Government resources were also required to process the data.

A significant development came in 1932 when the US Senate commissioned the Department of Commerce to compile statistics for US national income for 1929-1931. The aim was to ascertain just what had happened to US national income in the Great Depression. The Department of Commerce turned to Simon Kuznets at the National Bureau of Economic Research to complete the task. His report in January 1934 produced annual estimates of national income for 1929-32. The project continued, and by the end of the decade, regular estimates of US national income were being produced.

We have become so accustomed to national income statistics—including GDP (gross domestic product)—that it is easy to lose track of how complicated they are. Estimating national income involved much more than just adding up the numbers. In order to come up with national income estimates, it was necessary to establish a conceptual framework: to decide what was to be included and what was to be left out. For example, should government activity be part of national income, or should national income include only private incomes? If government activity is included, how should it be valued (that is a problem because many government activities are not bought and sold, and so prices do not exist). How do we value the services provided by roads and the police, or the value of services such as healthcare and education, when these are provided free by the state? Other issues include how retained corporate profits—profits that are not distributed to shareholders as dividends—are treated and how to handle the incomes of self-employed workers, for whom the division between wages and profits is often meaningless.

One issue, both a problem and an advantage, is that national income can be estimated in different ways. The obvious method is to add up all the incomes earned by people (wages, profits, and rents). Another one is to add up what everyone spends (consumption, investment, and any other types of spending). A third method is to add up the output produced in each sector of the economy, such as agriculture, mining, manufacturing, transportation, banking, and so on. A framework needs to be established for what is included and how different activities are valued so that these three sums are all consistent with each other.

An issue that was particularly important in the 1940s was the treatment of the government. Should the national accounts include what the government raised in taxation, or what it spent? When the budget was roughly balanced, it did not matter which was chosen, but during WWII, Federal spending rose dramatically, and most of the increase was funded by borrowing, not through taxes. This meant that it became important to measure what the federal government actually spent on goods and services, not just the part paid for by taxation.

Similar discussions took place in Britain, where Keynes, in the Treasury, was central to them. *How to Pay for the War* contained an appendix with national income estimates for Britain, covering a single year, 1938-9. He worked alongside younger colleagues, including James Meade (a former member of the Cambridge Circus) and Richard Stone, who, like Keynes, had entered the wartime Treasury. They were doing this because national income accounting proved to be crucial to wartime planning. Starting with an estimate of potential national income (assuming full employment), it is possible to estimate government consumption (needed for the war effort), to calculate what remains for private consumption. If the private sector's spending power exceeds this amount—if there is what was called an inflationary gap —it is possible to calculate how much income needs to be taken away from households, either through taxes or as compulsory saving, to prevent prices from being bid up. The concept underlying the analysis of inflation came to be known as the "inflationary gap"—the difference between aggregate demand and supply at full employment. Keynesian economics, worked out during the depression, had now become a theory of inflation with direct, practical application. Even Milton Friedman, a skeptic about the value of Keynesian policies during peacetime, considered the inflation gap theory useful in wartime. His reason was that in wartime, the objectives of policy were clear, and a market was not needed to ascertain them.

In the United States, estimates of national income were also used to gauge potential output that could be produced if there were full employment and resources were fully utilized. This was based on national income in 1929, the last year of full employment, adjusted to allow for subsequent population growth and increases in capacity. Essential civilian consumption was subtracted from that to give the volume of resources available for military production. Knowing the prices of various pieces of military equipment, it was then possible to calculate feasible levels of production. This "top-down" approach to economic planning differed greatly from the traditional "bottom-up" approach, focusing on the material inputs (copper, aluminum, steel, and so on) needed to make different types of equipment. It was the basis for the calculations made by Robert Nathan that formed the foundation for Roosevelt's "Victory Program."

In the United States, academic research did not stop completely, either in the period before the US entered the war, or afterwards. Indeed, thanks to its relevance to wartime planning, Keynesian economics was actively debated. Because of the war, many of the economists developing and applying Keynesian ideas were not in universities but were based in federal government agencies in Washington. They were therefore concerned not just with theory, but with how that theory would be translated into data analysis. This meant that Keynesian theory was developed in much closer contact with data analysis and practical policy problems than might have been the case in peacetime.

Nevertheless, theoretical research took place. During the war, the development of mathematical economics, a movement that got underway in the 1930s, continued, considerable stimulus being provided by the arrival of mathematically qualified immigrants from Europe who, because of their nationality, were not always eligible for government service. The process of making sense of Keynesian economics using small mathematical models that had begun as soon as the *General Theory* was published continued.

Keynes had written that he hoped to foment a revolution in the way the world thought about economic problems, and in 1945, Lawrence Klein, a young mathematically inclined economist, submitted a doctoral thesis at the Massachusetts Institute of Technology under the title of "The Keynesian Revolution." A revolution in economics had taken place, and it now had a name that stuck. However, a lot had happened to the world and to economic thinking in the nine years since *General Theory*'s publication. In particular, as has been explained, Keynesian ideas had been taken up by American economists, whose perspective on the subject was different from that of their British counterparts; and in both countries, the war had transformed the economic situation, requiring Keynesian ideas to be used in new ways.

We have already mentioned Keynes' wartime activity in relation to the development of the national accounts and designing measures to avoid inflation in Britain. However, Britain also faced the problem of raising the funds to pay for much-needed imports. Because factories had to be turned over to the war effort, the country could no longer earn money by exporting goods to the rest of the world. Shipping was also at a premium with a shortage of capacity and the danger of U-boat attacks. This required loans from the United States, without which Britain would have found it difficult, if not impossible, to continue fighting. The resources of the British Empire were vast, but dollars were also required, as well as American military hardware.

Despite his poor health following a heart attack in 1937, Keynes was involved in repeated negotiations with the American government, making several trips across the Atlantic.

Another major concern was the postwar economic order, for there was an awareness on all sides that one reason for the depth of the Great Depression was that the international trading system had collapsed in the 1930s. Countries imposed protection and devalued their currencies in order to give their industries a competitive advantage and stimulate production and employment. Few people wanted to return to such a situation, but the problem was what to put in its place.

A key question was what the international monetary system should look like. The Gold Standard had worked for a long time, but the stock of gold was limited, creating the likelihood that if currencies were convertible into gold, the world's money supply would not keep pace with production. The result would be a continual tendency to deflation —falling prices and stagnation, such as Britain had experienced in the 1920s. This tendency towards deflation would be made worse by the fact that countries with balance of payment deficits (importing more than exporting) would be under pressure to reduce demand in order to lower their imports to avoid running out of gold and foreign currency. In contrast, countries with surpluses would be under no pressure to take action: they could just let their reserves of foreign currency increase.

Such arguments imply that the world needs a reserve currency in addition to gold, so that the global supply of reserves can keep pace with world production. If this is to be an internationally issued reserve currency, there must be a body to issue it and to oversee the international financial system, ensuring that countries follow the rules. This raises the question about what powers such a body should have and what the rules governing the system must entail. Keynes produced one plan, and his American counterpart, Harry Dexter White, created another. It was generally agreed that exchange rates between different currencies should be fixed, but the question was how this should be achieved. Keynes was concerned with the asymmetry between surplus and deficit countries discussed in the previous paragraph, and the bias towards deflation that resulted. He argued for a system in which nations had the ability to borrow from the central organization, and that this body should be able to create currency that could be used as reserves. In contrast, the Americans were concerned that if resources were too readily available to deficit countries, they, the Americans, would be the ones who eventually paid the bill. Given the reality of political and economic power, the outcome, and the charter of the International Monetary Fund, it was established to regulate what came to be known as the Bretton Woods system. Named after the New Hampshire resort where the negotiations took place, it was closer to White's plan than to Keynes'.

AN AGE OF KEYNES?

Keynes recovered from his first heart attack, but not completely, and for the rest of his life, he was semi-invalid. With his transatlantic travel and involvement in very tense negotiations in the United States, he kept a punishing schedule, and Lydia sometimes had to hold him back for the sake of his health. He survived the war, but in 1946, while staying at his country home in Sussex, he went for a walk and suffered a fatal heart attack.

When Keynes died, it was clear that the United States was the center of world economics. American wealth and resources had no parallel anywhere else. American national income had risen dramatically during the war, while much of European industry had been destroyed. Even Britain, which was spared the destruction experienced in much of continental Europe, was effectively bankrupt, and because the economy had been mobilized for war, export markets had been lost. Not only was America much wealthier than Europe, but there were also more American economists than Europeans. This imbalance was reinforced by the enormous migration of economists, many of them Jews escaping persecution that had taken place in continental Europe, to the United States. The result was that, although those who were closely associated with Keynes during his lifetime—including Richard Kahn, Joan Robinson, James Meade, John Hicks, and Richard Stone—continued to develop his ideas, Keynesianism was increasingly associated with American economists. Alvin Hansen was one such example. His book, *A Guide to Keynes* (1953), provided an account of the *General Theory* that was shorter and easier to follow than Keynes' own book. Equally important was the younger generation of Keynesians, including Paul Samuelson, Franco Modigliani, James Tobin, and Lawrence Klein, for it was they who defined the way Keynesian economics looked in its heyday.

As we have mentioned, Samuelson was a graduate student at Harvard when the *General Theory* appeared, and he worked closely with Hansen from 1938 until the end of the war. During the war, he was one of the economists who worked on Keynesian economics, developing the theory and applying it to wartime problems. Afterwards, he wrote an introductory textbook, *Economics: an Introductory Analysis*, the first edition of which was published in 1948; it incorporated these ideas. Samuelson might describe the theory as "the modern national income approach," but its Keynesian pedigree was clear. His account of income determination centered on a simple diagram he had invented to explain the multiplier when he was analyzing Hansen's theory of the business cycle. It showed how, given the level of investment, the multiplier would determine the level of output and, hence, employment. It was a mechanical representation of Keynesian economics, in which interest rates, expectations, and other determinants of investment all happened offstage. One version of the diagram, depicting saving and investment, even appeared on the book's front cover and on its spine. This textbook was widely used, with millions of copies being sold (the 19th edition appeared in 2010), and it helped to define what Keynesian economics was for students in the 1950s and 1960s.

Another influential account of Keynesian economics was provided by Franco Modigliani, slightly younger than Samuelson, and an immigrant from Italy, who presented Keynesian theory in a way that related it to contemporary developments in the theory of markets. This was seen as a mathematically more rigorous explanation of Keynesian theory than either Keynes' own account or Hicks' IS-LM model. During the late 1940s and 1950s, it was followed by other attempts to provide accounts of the Keynesian system that conformed to the standards of rigor that economists increasingly expected. However, although most American economists probably favored Samuelson's and Modigliani's versions of Keynesianism, some remained attached to certain features of Keynes' arguments that were left out when they were translated into mathematics. They believed that crucial features of Keynes' own ideas, such as his focus on uncertainty, had been abandoned.

Lawrence Klein was Samuelson's first doctoral student, graduating, as was mentioned earlier, in 1945; he was the first to use the phrase "the Keynesian revolution" in print. However, his most important contribution to Keynesian economics came in the 1950s and 1960s, when he became the economist responsible, more than anyone else, for the construction of Keynesian econometric models containing numbers calculated from real-world data. They could be used to predict the amount by which policy changes would affect key variables and were useful in generating precise numerical forecasts. To understand what this means, note that models based on consumption functions such as $C = a + bY$, where a and b are unknown coefficients, are purely theoretical. This equation says that if income increases, consumption also rises by a certain amount, but unless we know the value of the coefficient b, we do not know how much it increases. To convert a theoretical equation into one that can be used to generate quantitative forecasts, the coefficients a and b have to be replaced with real numbers, which will, of course, be different for every country to which the theory is applied. They have to be calculated from real-world data on consumption and income. In addition, to be at all realistic, consumption functions need to be much more complicated than $C = a + bY$, bringing in other variables such as households' holdings of financial assets and property, rates of interest, and perhaps the availability of credit. They also have to take into account the lags that may be involved between changes in income and households' decisions to change their spending (if income rises, households may take time to decide that they can afford to spend more). It is also possible that consumption of durable goods (such as washing machines and automobiles) may depend on factors that are quite different from consumption of food and other non-durable goods; if so, then it may be necessary to have different consumption equations for different types of consumption. Similar complications apply to other components of aggregate demand, such as investment, imports, and exports. The result is that a model that can be used to answer questions such as, "By how much will national income increase next year?" or "If the government raises the rate of income tax from 20% to 22%, by how much will national income be reduced?" will generally become much more complicated than anything Keynes proposed, even if the basic structure of the theory is Keynesian.

Keynesian econometric models, developed by a community of economists to whom Klein was central, were essentially elaborations of the theory Keynes had proposed in the *General Theory*. It was assumed that aggregate demand determined output and employment, and that to explain aggregate demand, it had to be subdivided into its various components, each of which would be explained by a different equation. There would typically also be variables explaining how prices would rise as the economy approached full employment and resources became scarce, so that the models explained inflation as well as employment. Because they were typically developed to guide government policy, such models often had very detailed descriptions of taxes and the various interventions government or central banks could make in the economy. For example, the Federal Reserve might wish to know what the implications of some complicated monetary policy operation would be for the wider economy, and only a model with a very detailed monetary sector could answer this. By the 1960s, as electronic computers became more powerful and more widely available, such models, which were typically the result of work by large teams of researchers—economists' equivalent of "big science"—could have hundreds and in some cases thousands of equations, many of which had to be estimated from data.

There was a widely held belief that there must be no return to the world of the Great Depression with the mass unemployment that scarred those years. However, there were differences of opinion over how to achieve this. In the United States, the Employment Act of 1946 set up the Council of Economic Advisers and placed economic advice at the heart of government, but it stopped short of the commitment to ensuring full employment that some of its supporters had wanted. During the Eisenhower administration, from 1952 to 1960, policy was in the hands of economists, such as Arthur Burns, who were cautious in their attitude towards Keynes. There was also considerable opposition, especially in conservative quarters, to high levels of government spending, and there was an even greater fear of government deficits. In 1960, the leadership of the Council passed to Walter Heller and later Gardner Ackley, who had fewer doubts about Keynesian policies and sought to regulate demand to avoid the recessions seen under Eisenhower. This was the high point of Keynesianism in American policymaking and in academia. Samuelson and his colleagues were critical of the Eisenhower administration for overseeing no fewer than three recessions in an eight-year period, each deeper than the previous one. To reverse this trend, the Kennedy administration, following the advice of Samuelson and Heller's Council of Economic Advisers, implemented a tax cut, which they believed was the most effective way to stimulate consumption and aggregate demand in order to achieve a higher level of employment. Samuelson's argument for tax cuts rather than expenditure increases was that democratically elected policymakers should determine the level and type of expenditure (roads, schools, hospitals, warships, aircraft, and so on), based on what they believed society needed, and that taxation should then be set to generate the appropriate level of aggregate demand. This would be high enough to avoid large-scale unemployment, but not so high that it would generate inflation.

In Europe, the situation was more varied. Keynesianism dominated policymaking in Britain, though there were doubts about how effective such policies were. Some economists claimed that, because the government often got the timing of policy initiatives wrong, its effects failed to stabilize the level of activity. German policy was based on the "Social Market", which was far from Keynesian in its inspiration, and in other countries, such as the Netherlands and France, planning mechanisms were far stronger than in either Britain or Germany. Keynesianism was predominantly an Anglo-American phenomenon in a world where other countries, from Latin America to Africa, India, and the Far East, were concerned with economic development rather than with sustaining aggregate demand.

5
THE REACTION AGAINST KEYNESIANISM

THE END OF THE GOLDEN AGE

In the 1970s, there was a turn against Keynesianism. The tax cut for which Kennedy was responsible achieved its goal of reducing unemployment, and by the mid-1960s, Keynesian economists such as Samuelson began warning about the dangers of inflation. However, after Kennedy's assassination, Lyndon Johnson was committed to his "Great Society" program and to reducing poverty. The result was that domestic spending increased. So too did spending on the Vietnam War, which was escalating. Keynesian economists, including ones on the Council of Economic Advisers, warned Johnson that he needed to raise taxes if he were to avoid inflation, but taxes were not increased. The situation came to a head in the early 1970s, after Johnson had been succeeded by Richard Nixon, when the high level of demand caused commodity prices to rise, pushing up the rate of inflation to levels previously seen only in wartime.

The climax came in 1973 when the Yom Kippur War between Israel and its Arab neighbors resulted in an embargo on oil supplies to countries supporting Israel, and the Organization of Petroleum Exporting Countries (OPEC) formed an effective cartel, limiting the supply of oil and causing a threefold rise in its price. This was a shock such as the world economy had not experienced since World War II. It had multiple effects, involving blows to both aggregate demand and supply. The demand shock came about because the rise in oil prices transferred massive wealth to oil-exporting countries, notably Saudi Arabia and the Gulf states, at the expense of oil-importing nations, which had to pay much more for their oil. This transfer of wealth was immediate, but oil-exporting countries did not immediately increase their spending. The result was a massive reduction in global aggregate demand. There were schemes to recycle so-called "petrodollars" to countries that needed to borrow dollars to fund their spending, but this could not happen overnight. The embargo caused disruption by creating physical shortages of oil. The rise in oil prices was also a shock to supply because such a large increase in the price of energy rendered a lot of technology obsolete, as it was uneconomic to operate at high energy prices. The symbol of this was the demise of the large gas-guzzling automobiles that had been common in America in the 1950s and 1960s, but it was a much more wide-ranging phenomenon, affecting large sections of industry. It was as though a large slice of the world's capital stock had been wiped out. Production costs rose dramatically. The result was that the world was plunged, very quickly, into depression at the same time as inflation rose dramatically. This was the new phenomenon of "stagflation"—a combination of unemployment and inflation. The rise in costs and in the prices of imported materials, notably oil, produced inflation, and the collapse in aggregate demand created unemployment.

This was a situation that Keynesian economics could easily explain; indeed, Keynesian economists had been warning about potential problems for several years, but they could not provide a simple remedy. Keynesian policy, as the term was understood, involved using monetary or fiscal policy to raise aggregate demand when unemployment was unacceptably high, and to lower aggregate demand when the problem was inflation. Where both inflation and unemployment were rising, calculating the optimal policy was difficult, involving balancing the costs of inflation against the costs of unemployment. For example, Samuelson regarded high employment as the priority, taking the view that inflation should be tackled later. It was wrong to use high unemployment to bring down inflation because doing this would place the burden on the poor, and in particular on black youths, amongst whom unemployment was very high. In some countries, including the United States and Britain, governments tried to cut the Gordian knot by means of "incomes policy," a term that covered policies ranging from "moral suasion" and "wage-price guideposts" to statutory controls on price and wage changes. Such policies proved able to reduce inflation in the very short term, interrupting wage-price spirals that were getting out of control, but they generally created problems in the longer term and failed to provide an adequate solution.

This is the context in which governments turned to "monetarism," the doctrine that stability was best achieved by ensuring that the money supply grew at a predictable, ideally constant rate. It was based on the quantity theory of money, the theory that Keynes, following his teacher Marshall, had used in the 1920s to reach policy conclusions that differed greatly from Friedman's, but which he had decisively rejected in the *General Theory*. In the 1950s and 1960s, the quantity theory had fallen out of favor because there appeared to be little connection between the money supply and the price level. Economists had come to believe that the supply of credit, something that depended on the operation of the entire financial system, and which could not be expressed as a single number, was more important than the money supply alone. For example, the ability of a business or a household to buy goods and services might depend as much on its ability to borrow as on the amount it has in the bank, but overdraft facilities and the ability to obtain trade credit would not bear any relationship to the money supply.

In the late 1940s, Milton Friedman, recently arrived at the University of Chicago, began a project organized through the National Bureau of Economic Research to rehabilitate the quantity theory of money. As part of this project, he challenged the notion that the multiplier—a concept central to Keynesian economics—was sufficiently stable for policy analysis, arguing that the so-called "velocity of circulation", a key variable in the quantity theory of money, was more stable. He produced evidence purporting to show that changes in the money supply were a better predictor of changes in spending than were changes in investment. And crucially, he argued that the lags involved in policy were so unpredictable that any attempt to use policy changes to stabilize the economy was doomed to fail. A particularly important piece of research, conducted together with Anna Schwartz, was *A Monetary History of the United States, 1867-*

1960 (1963). Amongst other claims, this book argued that, contrary to what was commonly believed, the Great Depression did not show that monetary policy was impotent. On the contrary, incompetent monetary policy, which had allowed the money supply to collapse, was responsible for turning a normal cyclical downturn into a major catastrophe. Paradoxically, the episode showed how powerful monetary policy was.

During the 1950s and 1960s, Keynesians repeatedly challenged Friedman's claims, including Modigliani and Tobin, and he frequently appeared in debates with Samuelson. Keynesians believed they could counter many of his arguments, but support grew for the quantity theory and for the policy prescriptions that were, from 1968, described as monetarism. Paradoxically, Friedman's theoretical approach was in many ways closer to that of Keynes himself than to the mathematical theorizing favored by many of his contemporaries. He preferred using simple models as a framework within which to structure his thinking, rather than favoring the more complex theoretical and empirical models used by Keynesians.

In the 1970s, Friedman's ideas became much more popular and, even though they were not always followed, Nixon sought his advice and from governments across the world. (For example, Friedman was very critical of Nixon's turn to incomes policy.) The dramatic rise in inflation during the early 1970s, which had been accompanied by a comparable rise in the money supply, appeared to provide support for the quantity theory. Faced with stagnation after 1973, monetarism—the notion that policymakers should not target unemployment, as Keynesians argued, but should target the growth rate of the money supply—became attractive to policymakers because it offered guidance in what were otherwise puzzling circumstances. The myth developed that Keynesian economists, some of whom had been warning about the dangers of inflation since the mid-1960s, had not anticipated the effects of the policies that had been pursued since that time. There was a move away from Keynesian policies, with Keynesian economists being blamed for the decisions of an administration that had failed to implement the policies they said were necessary to avoid inflation.

However, the challenge from Friedman and monetarism was not the only challenge to Keynesianism in the 1970s. There was also a perception that the large forecasting models used by Keynesian economists to design monetary and fiscal policies had failed. The 1973-4 oil crisis was an unprecedented shock to the world economy, both in its scale and its type. As has been explained, it involved a supply shock as well as a demand shock. Keynesian econometric models had been developed to explain a world that was very different in that there had been no large supply shocks, and, not surprisingly, they did not fit the new circumstances well. They needed to be modified to cope with the new reality. In particular, they had to be extended to analyze the supply of goods and services as well as demand, something that had not been necessary in the comparatively stable world of the previous 30 years. There had been upheavals, such as the Korean War, but nothing like the shocks of the mid-1970s. The new circumstances raised the question of whether the changes required were inevitable modifications that any model would need in order to cope with the new situation, or whether they were an indication that there was something fundamentally wrong with the models. Keynesian modelers claimed the former: that any model has to be based on what has happened in the past, and that whenever something unprecedented happens, models will need to be adapted. In contrast, Monetarists argued that Keynesian models were inherently flawed. The largest models were much too big to be developed by a single economist and were produced by large teams of researchers, with different economists responsible for different parts of the model. For example, one team might estimate consumption equations, while another, perhaps in a different university or a different government department, developed a model of the labor market, and yet another team worked out the financial sector. The result was that the various parts of the model, having been developed independently, might not fit together very well. Monetarist critics claimed that such models would inevitably be inconsistent and doomed to failure. Simpler, smaller models were the way forward.

CHALLENGING THE THEORY

At the same time as Friedman argued that Keynesian theories could not explain the data and that Keynesian policies were bound to fail, other economists challenged the theoretical foundations of Keynesian economics. Keynes had based his theory on accounts of individual behavior involving social psychology, generalizing about behavior that was derived from experience and common sense. This meant that, as economists increasingly adopted mathematical methods and constructed more formal theories, his ideas looked increasingly imprecise and dated, for he was discussing ideas that were difficult to model formally.

There was a similar problem with Keynes' conception of

markets. It would have made sense for Keynes to assume that competition was "imperfect"—that individual businesses had some power to control the prices at which they sold their products; that they had a degree of monopoly power. This would have made it much easier for him to explain the existence of unemployment. But he did not. If he had assumed imperfect competition, critics would have challenged his claim to be undermining the traditional theory, which was based on perfect competition—the notion that individual businesses are too small relative to the market to have any market power and, as a result, are price-takers, who must accept market prices, whatever they are.

In the 1950s and 1960s, many Keynesian economists, such as Samuelson, followed Keynes in using verbal reasoning to discuss issues that were not captured in their mathematics. One reason for this was that they took it for granted that important markets were imperfectly competitive, and it was difficult to construct mathematical models of markets in which there were very few participants, each of whom had some market power. Everyone knew there existed large and powerful labor unions and that, through collective bargaining and the threat of industrial action, they could influence the wages earned by their members. And there were large corporations dominating product markets—what the economist J. K. Galbraith called the technostructure. These corporations, Galbraith and others argued, were not subject to market discipline but had the power and resources to engage in extensive planning, using advertising to manipulate markets.

However, though many economists, especially those engaged in policy analysis, adopted methods that echoed those employed by Keynes, economists increasingly took the view that all the steps in an argument should be mathematically rigorous. This typically implied the use of higher-level mathematics and symbolic representation rather than verbal reasoning. Using these tools forced economists to make simplifying assumptions because otherwise, the theory would be too difficult to work with. The consequence was that, instead of Keynes' accounts of the social psychology of consumption or investment, they started with the assumption that firms maximize profits, that consumers choose the best out of all the alternatives available to them, and that markets are perfectly competitive. It also became common to work with the simplification that all individuals are the same, so that consumers as a whole behave like a single consumer, but millions of times larger.

There were valid reasons many economists went down this route of constructing theories that were mathematically more rigorous. Using mathematics made it much easier to be certain that results followed logically from the assumptions that had been made, and that no unstated assumptions had been smuggled into the analysis. It also made it possible to derive results that would otherwise have been hidden. And there are legitimate reasons for wanting macroeconomic models to be grounded on assumptions about individual behavior—to have what were called "microfoundations."

However, it proved difficult to use such theories to explain the existence of involuntary unemployment. The assumption of optimizing agents and perfectly competitive markets led inexorably to the conclusion that people are unemployed because they have decided not to work, perhaps because they dislike the available jobs, or because they think they are entitled to a higher wage than they are being offered, or because they find living on unemployment benefits more attractive than working for a living. Building models describing people who wanted to work at the going wage rate but could not get a job was much more difficult. Keynes' explanations of why cuts in wages would not eliminate unemployment increasingly seemed unsatisfactory.

This prompted some economists to search for better microfoundations for Keynesian economics. Two examples illustrate this. The first is Axel Leijonhufvud, whose work was widely cited in the 1970s. He started from the assumption that, except for certain financial markets, markets would not be in equilibrium with supply equal to demand all the time, for the simple reason that it took businesses time to change their prices and production schedules. In a constantly changing world, knowledge is limited. Moreover, if markets are not in equilibrium, some people's plans will inevitably not be realized, forcing them to revise their decisions. The result, he showed, could easily be unemployment. Workers cut back on their spending because they cannot find jobs, and firms do not employ them because they cannot sell the goods they produce. The economy might therefore get stuck in a situation with high unemployment.

This explanation of Keynesian economics was based on a view of markets as information-processing systems that Hayek had formulated in the 1930s when he was working on the problem of central planning versus the market economy, but it turns his argument on its head. Whereas Hayek had used it to argue that central planning was impossible and that decisions needed to be left to the market, Leijonhufvud used such arguments to explain why a capitalist economy might sometimes fail.

The second example is Edmund Phelps, who developed more formal, highly influential models of information and market equilibrium. He talked about how misperceptions about what was happening to prices and wages might explain unemployment. In these theories, workers are choosing the best opportunities available to them, but because they have incorrect information, they make decisions that cause them to be unemployed. However, though Phelps was explaining unemployment, the problem that motivated Keynes, he was creating what were technically theories of voluntary unemployment. His theories were influential because, unlike Leijonhufvud, who relied on verbal analysis, Phelps was constructing rigorous mathematical models that had seemingly great potential for development.

It was a short step from here to the conclusion that involuntary unemployment, a concept fundamental to Keynesian economics, was theoretically incoherent. Phelps did not draw this conclusion, but some economists, such as Robert Lucas, did. Because they reached "classical" conclusions, this approach came to be called "new classical" economics. The search for what they deemed to be more rigorous microfoundations led the new classical economists to reject Keynesian economics. Their theories were fundamentally different from Friedman's because his methods remained much closer to Keynes'. But the new classical economists shared Friedman's repudiation of demand-management policies and, like him, they endorsed non-intervention, policy rules, and "free markets."

Lucas was also important because, in 1976, he provided a

very influential theoretical explanation of why Keynesian macro-econometric models had failed in the 1970s. The problem, he argued, was that Keynesian models were based on observed past behavior, and there was no reason to believe that this behavior would stay the same when circumstances changed. The result was that if policy changed, people's behavior would change as well, and these correlations and the parameters of the models would also be modified, rendering the models useless for policy analysis. In other words, the apparent failure of Keynesian models was not accidental—it arose not because the modelers had made mistakes, but because it was inherent in the methods by which the models had been constructed. To be robust to policy changes, and hence to be usable for policy analysis, models had to be constructed very differently.

In addition, around the 1970s, an increasing number of economists took up the analysis of "government failure." There were two main arguments here. The first was that, in the same way, private agents had limited information, governments would often have too little information to design effective stabilization policies. They were therefore likely to make mistakes, destabilizing the economy rather than stabilizing it. The second was that the government was run by politicians and bureaucrats, who followed their own objectives. Politicians, at least in democratic societies, were seen as motivated not by the public good but by the search for electoral success. Some argued this would bias them towards excessively inflationary policies, for increases in spending and tax cuts are always more popular than spending cuts and tax increases. There could, therefore, be no assurance that, even if economists could design an effective stabilization policy, it would be implemented. Better, it was argued, to remove politicians' discretion over policy by legislating rules, such as Friedman's rule of a constant growth rate of the money supply, or a requirement that government budgets be balanced, either of which would make Keynesian demand management impossible.

Economists who remained sympathetic to Keynesian ways of thinking responded to these criticisms in different ways. Some rejected the type of theorizing represented by Lucas, claiming that it could never do justice to crucial Keynesian insights, such as the pervasiveness of uncertainty, that could not be reduced to calculations of probability. A more influential group, including Phelps, used the new, more rigorous ways of theorizing to develop models that supported Keynesian conclusions, finding reasons market mechanisms would be unable to eliminate unemployment. Imperfect competition, costs of changing prices, and limitations on the information available to households and firms could all interfere with the operation of the price mechanism, creating unemployment. The economists who developed such theories came to be called "new Keynesian" economists, though, as both groups modified their theories and tried to explain the data, the distinction between new classical and new Keynesian economics became increasingly blurred. A minority of economists protested that Keynesian insights had been abandoned, but, for many economists, economics had moved on; they believed, rightly or wrongly, that Keynesian insights had been incorporated into models that were superior to those in use in the so-called Keynesian era.

THE MORALITY OF GOVERNMENT INTERVENTION

By the end of the 1970s, therefore, Keynesianism was widely perceived to have failed on several fronts. Keynesian policies were believed to lie at the root of the economic turmoil that engulfed the world after 1973; the policy guidance provided by Keynesian economics in a world of stagflation was not clear, and many economists thought Keynesian theory was misconceived. Perhaps more importantly, however, the notion that government should take responsibility for economic welfare, actively intervening to do things that otherwise would not get done, was questioned. This was a challenge not just to Keynesianism as it existed in the 1960s and to the theory he had developed in the *General Theory*, but also to the moral arguments Keynes had presented in *Economic Consequences of the Peace* and in the 1920s. Government, it was believed, should play a much more limited role.

This is where Hayek entered the story in a significant way. As was explained in Chapter 3, there was a very brief period, in 1930-31, when Hayek and Keynes argued publicly over business cycle theory. They never resolved their differences. However, to portray this as an ongoing debate between Keynes and Hayek is very misleading. Hayek dropped out of the argument, turning instead to the problem of central planning and arguments for the superiority of capitalism over socialism—a position on which he and Keynes agreed. They became close during World War II, when the London School of Economics moved to Cambridge, and, as liberals, they faced a common enemy. Keynes arranged for Hayek to have the right to dine at King's College, Cambridge, and the two of them socialized at weekends when Keynes was there. When Hayek brought out the book that made him famous, *The Road to Serfdom* (1944), he naturally sent a copy to Keynes, who replied appreciatively. He picked out a passage in which Hayek had written about the importance of the profit motive and capitalism:

> The younger generation of today has grown up in a world in which in school and press the spirit of commercial enterprise has been represented as disreputable and the making of profit as immoral. . . . the daily experience of the University teacher leaves little doubt that as a result of anti-capitalist propaganda values have already altered far in advance of the change in institutions which has yet taken place in this country. The question is whether by changing our institutions to satisfy the new demands, we shall not unwittingly destroy values which we rate still higher.*

Keynes argued that this passage could not be bettered and that he agreed with it.

From the 1940s to the 1960s, Hayek stopped working as an economist, turning to psychology and political philosophy, among other topics. His importance after the war, therefore, lies not in his economics but in the major role he played in the revival of conservatism and opposition to Keynesian political philosophy as it had come to be understood in the 1950s and 1960s.

Opposition to Keynesianism, defined as a political philosophy rather than a purely economic theory, did not grow just by accident. Some businessmen had welcomed

---

* Hayek The Road to Serfdom (Routledge 1944), 97.

Roosevelt's New Deal, with the opportunities it provided, while others were hostile, seeing it as creeping socialism that threatened to undermine the American way of life. By contemporary standards, the postwar consensus about policy was comparatively liberal (in the American sense). America never opted for a European-style welfare state, but even under Eisenhower, the degree of intervention was sufficiently large to be seen as threatening by many conservatives. Kennedy and Johnson took that a step further. There were, therefore, businesses and private foundations to support conservative thinkers who would challenge accepted views.

Hayek believed that changing this consensus had to be a long-term project and, supported by sympathetic businessmen, he took several steps to do this. In 1947, he organized a conference of social scientists committed to developing a philosophy of freedom. It is natural to speculate that, given his wartime friendship with Hayek and his Liberal politics (as that term was understood in Europe), Keynes might have been invited to attend—had he been alive and had his health permitted. This meeting took place in Switzerland, bringing together a group dominated by economists from Britain, continental Europe, and the United States. Significantly, the American contingent included Milton Friedman and some of his colleagues from Chicago. The outcome was the formation of the Mont Pelerin Society, named after the resort in which the meeting had taken place. This was to serve as the center of a network for academics and others committed to developing a philosophy of freedom, or of liberalism, as the term is understood in Europe.

A few years later, believing that the most effective way to change thinking was to focus on what he called dealers in secondhand ideas—to focus on organizations that could translate ideas into terms that policymakers and the public would understand—Hayek helped to found the Institute of Economic Affairs in London. It served as a think tank committed to the development and propagation of free-market ideas. Keynesianism, which implied a significant role for the government, was a major target of such organizations, along with the welfare state, anti-monopoly legislation, minimum wage laws, and many other forms of government intervention. Technical economic arguments were also brought to bear on the problem, but the critique of interventionism was as much political and philosophical as economic.

In 1950, Hayek, who had by then moved away from mainstream economics, left the London School of Economics for a position in an interdisciplinary unit called the Committee on Social Thought at the University of Chicago. He was never considered for the Economics Department because, even though his politics would have been congenial to Friedman, he simply did not have the profile expected of an economist in the postwar era.

In the economics department, Friedman was responsible not just for developing monetarism, but also for critiques of government intervention in a wide range of areas. He was an early supporter of flexible exchange rates—the idea that exchange rates should be allowed to fluctuate in response to changes in supply and demand for foreign currency; he was a critic of rent controls and of many other types of intervention. However, although Friedman was an economist, his opposition to Keynes centered on Keynes' political philosophy as much as on his economic reasoning. As he put it, Keynes' answer to economic problems was to have the government solve them, and for the government to put intellectuals in charge—two steps that Friedman, brought up in a very different environment, refused to accept.

In the 1950s and for much of the 1960s, the position held by Hayek and Friedman was in a minority. Their ideas were supported by Presidential candidate Barry Goldwater in 1964, but Johnson resoundingly defeated him. However, around 1980, a more sympathetic generation of political figures came to power, of whom the most important were Ronald Reagan and Margaret Thatcher. They were prepared to reject Keynesianism, both as an economic doctrine and as a political philosophy, with a consistency that their predecessors had not shown.

FINANCIAL CRISIS AND AFTER

From the late 1980s until the beginning of the 21st century, the United States and several other countries experienced a period of steady growth, with a low and stable rate of inflation, and without mass unemployment. The business cycle, a feature of capitalist economies throughout history, appeared to have been tamed. The policies on which this was based were far from those advocated by Keynes. They involved using monetary policy—control over interest rates—to target inflation. If inflation threatened to rise too far, interest rates were raised, and if they fell below a pre-announced target, they were lowered. Rather than urging governments to take responsibility for economic outcomes, decisions over the implementation of policy were taken away from politicians and given to unelected central bankers. The theory behind this was that politicians would abuse their authority for their own ends. More concerned with their prospects for re-election than with the interests of the country, politicians would take measures likely to be popular, creating a bias towards expansionary policy. These policies, supplemented with measures to enhance the freedom of the private sector to take initiatives, notably deregulation of the financial system, were very un-Keynesian.

The result was that Keynesian economics appeared to be dead. There were, of course, crises in parts of the world, notably the economic disaster that struck Russia and many ex-communist countries after the collapse of the Soviet Union, and the East Asian financial crisis that began in 1997, but these could be explained in terms specifically related to those countries. They were not perceived as raising questions about economic theory in general. If there were lessons to be learned, they were not related to Keynes.

Unfortunately, although the growth of output, unemployment, and inflation rate may have stabilized, the same was not true for asset prices—the prices of equities and property. In 1987, there had been a dramatic stock market crash, widely linked to the growth of computerized trading and activity that would not have been possible without the liberalization of markets that had taken place during the 1970s and 1980s. In 1998, there was the spectacular collapse of the hedge fund, Long Term Capital Management, followed in the early 2000s by the Dot-com bubble, which saw a boom in shares in newly created internet companies, which also suffered a spectacular collapse. House price inflation was much more unstable than general inflation, and a boom developed in house prices between 2004 and 2006. During the boom, lending increased dramatically, especially to subprime borrowers; as a result, when house prices stopped rising, as they did in early 2007, many borrowers found themselves in financial trouble and defaulted on their mortgages. The problem was that these mortgages were no longer held by the companies that made the loans, but had been re-sold to other financial institutions, including some of the largest banks, and so defaults threatened the stability of the entire financial system, not simply the companies that had made the loans. The financial system seized up across the world, and global markets lurched into recession.

The fear was that there would be a return to the mass unemployment of the 1930s. To avoid this scenario, there was a return to policies that had been rejected for the preceding two decades. Governments poured money into supporting the financial system, important financial institutions that had gotten into trouble were nationalized, and there was large-scale government spending to support production and employment. There was a Keynesian stimulus to sustain aggregate demand and avoid a massive rise in unemployment. In the United States, the Economic Stimulus Act of 2008 provided for tax cuts of around $100 billion, and further stimulus was provided by legislation the following year. There was a flurry of interest in Keynes, as even conservative economists took him seriously for the first time. Numerous books on Keynes were published. He became relevant again.

This interest in Keynes, however, was not to last. Within a couple of years, governments got concerned with levels of public debt and controlling deficits to bring debt levels down. Given that there was no desire to raise taxes, for it was believed that this would damage incentives to work and to undertake investment, this meant a return to austerity, to cuts in public spending. Although the effects of austerity were felt in many countries, the most dramatic instance was probably Greece, due to its membership in the Eurozone, dominated by Germany.

The world avoided a repeat of the Great Depression. However, the result was not the return to Keynesian ways of thinking that many had hoped for, but a return to older concerns with austerity and balancing government budgets. Reasons for this no doubt vary between countries, but there was a deliberate attempt by economists and organizations associated with the Mont Pelerin Society to present the crisis as a problem created by governments rather than as a problem inherent in free or inadequately regulated markets. In some countries, a strategy of blaming the crisis on governments was politically advantageous. For example, in Britain, it was politically useful for the Conservative opposition to blame the fiscal deficit on the alleged profligacy of the Labour government, rather than linking it to the global financial crisis, making a case for austerity.

There was concern that rapidly rising levels of government debt would lead to inflation. However, given that inflation was generally below Central Banks' target levels, and that interest rates were very low, it is hard to see any real reason for inflation to be such a concern. It, therefore, seems likely that fear of deficits was used as a justification for cutting welfare provisions and other government-funded programs that conservative governments wished to eliminate for other reasons.

The turn to austerity could be seen as a reprise of ideas that had been prevalent in the early 1930s, against which Keynes was arguing when he made the case for public works spending. It was also a rejection of the ideas of postwar

Keynesians, such as Samuelson, who repeatedly claimed that government deficits were not necessarily a cause for concern. Keynes was forgotten almost as quickly as he had been rediscovered.

The result of this return to policies of austerity was that, in many countries, recovery from the recession was extremely slow. In response, Lawrence Summers, Harvard Professor of Economics and former Secretary of the Treasury and Chief Economist at the World Bank, revived the idea of "secular stagnation"—the notion that there was a long-term tendency for economies to generate too little aggregate demand to allow a return to normal rates of growth. This idea goes back not to Keynes (though there are some suggestions in this direction in an article he wrote on population growth) but to Alvin Hansen and some of his students who, as was explained in Chapter 4, had developed the concept in the late 1930s and 1940s to explain what was happening to the US economy. Summers explained it differently. However, this theory is deeply rooted in Keynesian economics and can legitimately be seen as its extension. To understand Summers' theory, we need to backtrack a little.

Knut Wicksell, on whose work Keynes had drawn in his *Treatise on Money*, the book he abandoned before writing the *General Theory,* explained inflation and deflation in terms of a difference between two rates of interest: the market rate of interest and the natural rate of interest. The market rate of interest is self-explanatory: it is the rate of interest actually charged on loans by the banking system. The natural rate will lead to a balance between saving and investment in the economy, and it is related to the rate of return that entrepreneurs can get by investing in physical capital goods such as plants and machinery. If the natural rate is higher than the market rate, entrepreneurs will find it profitable to borrow from the banking system and invest in real productive activity; investment will be higher than savings. The economy will grow and, once full employment is achieved, there will be a tendency towards rising prices.

What had happened since the global financial crisis, Summers argued, was that the natural rate of interest had fallen below the rate of interest charged by the banking system. The natural rate might even be negative. This is a serious problem because there is generally a limit to how low the market rate of interest can fall. The obvious limit is zero, which arises because people always have the option to hold cash: if interest rates were negative, people would have an incentive to hold cash instead—hence talk of a zero lower bound (ZLB) to interest. Worse than this, Keynes pointed out that there might be what he called a "liquidity trap" in which, even at a positive rate of interest, people preferred holding cash to bonds, because they were worried about bond prices falling when interest rates eventually rose. (When interest rates rise, bond prices fall, and vice versa.) Either way, because of a liquidity trap or the zero lower bound on interest rates, a negative natural rate of interest implies a tendency toward depression. Monetary policy, which operates by lowering interest rates, would be powerless to do anything about it, implying a need for fiscal stimulus—for Keynesian policies.

6

KEYNES' LEGACY

CHANGING INTERPRETATIONS

Economists hold very different attitudes towards Keynes. For many, he is simply a figure from the past who contributed to the economics we have today, but whose work has been superseded by more modern economics. Many of them see no need to engage seriously with the economist himself or with his ideas. Whatever their politics, and whether they agree with his stance on policy, they take the view that his theorizing does not meet the standards of rigor necessary to take his work seriously—his theory, for instance, was not presented with mathematical precision. Such economists are likely to use the term "Keynesian" as a shorthand to refer to certain positions on economic theory or policy. This means, for example, that if modern theory leads to the conclusion that Keynes needed to assume wages were sticky on the basis that otherwise his explanation of unemployment would not make sense, they associate Keynesian economics with the assumption of wage stickiness, without reference to what Keynes himself said about the subject.

At the other pole are economists who are convinced that the world needs to return to Keynes' ideas, arguing that subsequent generations of economists abandoned his key insights. What passed for Keynesian economics in the postwar period—the models of Samuelson, Modigliani, and Tobin—was, to use Joan Robinson's much-quoted phrase, "bastard Keynesianism." According to such economists, we need to recover the original Keynes—the true Keynesian theory. It is possible to point to Keynes' skepticism about early econometric modeling and to conclude that the efforts of Klein and others to formulate Keynesian forecasting models were misconceived. Another perspective comes from taking seriously Keynes' remarks about the need to analyze a world in which we know next to nothing about the future; given that most translations of Keynes into mathematical models necessarily turn his theory into something more manageable, this can easily lead to the conclusion that postwar Keynesians missed the point of what Keynes was saying.

Economists are also divided on Keynes' policy prescriptions. As we saw in Chapter 5, some reject Keynes' policy prescriptions and see his arguments as thinly veiled arguments for increasing the role of the state and government interference. Often, such a perspective is based on the view that his policies were tried in the 1960s and that events of the 1970s proved them to be flawed. Even if one concedes that there is a theoretical case for interventionist policies, it is possible to argue that governments cannot be trusted to take appropriate action, either because the task of working out how to manage the economy is impossibly complicated, or because political pressures will create a bias towards policies that will generate excessive inflation. Opposition to Keynes is political as well as economic, and it is sometimes hard to be sure which one is dominant.

It should be clear by now that this book is arguing for none of these positions. Its primary focus is to understand Keynes: we should not rely on stereotypes, because, whether we agree with his ideas, Keynes was a much more interesting thinker than modern commentary gives him credit for. Chapters 1 to 3 presented a short overview of Keynes' life and work, trying to place him in the context of his own time. A key theme is that Keynes was arguing two cases. The first was the moral argument that policymakers had a responsibility to make decisions that would improve the way the economy worked. The second was that the government should focus on those things that, if the government did not do them, would not get done at all. The most important example of such a problem was managing investment and saving in the interests of society as a whole. If the government did not take responsibility for managing aggregate demand, no one else would. The Great Depression showed that if the government did nothing, market forces would not ensure that aggregate demand was high enough to achieve full employment. Responsible management of aggregate demand was also necessary in wartime, when the problem was too much demand, not too little.

The way Keynes thought about these issues changed because the policy problems Britain faced also shifted significantly over the course of his career. He started by becoming an expert on international finance in the context of the problems posed by the British Empire in India, from which he was able to progress to wartime financial problems. After World War I, the first major problem he tackled was the consequences of the peace treaty, again an issue of international finance. For most of the 1920s, he was concerned with the return to the gold standard and then solving the problem of unemployment that the return at an inappropriate exchange rate had caused. In the 1930s, of course, he turned to the problem of mass unemployment. Although his most famous theory, in which he challenged conventional economic thinking most profoundly, was developed in the context of world depression and mass unemployment, its first application came in World War II, when Britain faced the opposite problem of full employment and potential inflation (Keynes had tried to persuade Roosevelt but had not succeeded; the New Deal was not Keynesian in its inspiration). These changes in the problems he faced formed the background to the evolution of his thinking.

In tackling these difficulties, for many years Keynes used conventional theories innovatively, but later on, he developed his own theory that was then taken over and developed by others. In the early 1920s, he relied on the quantity theory of money, developed by his teacher Marshall. Towards the end of the decade, he tried to develop a new theory of money and the economy. His terminology of "fundamental equations" shows that he was trying to explain theoretically what had gone wrong. However, he quickly became aware, mainly through the criticisms of his Cambridge colleagues, that his theory was not a success, for the argument on which it was based contained a fatal inconsistency. So he immediately developed the theory with which his name is now associated, presenting this as a revolutionary break from the past. Whether we agree with this assessment (something on which there is scope for debate), one thing that remained constant was his moral position: his belief that policymakers should face up to their responsibilities, and that saving and investment decisions lay at the heart of economic problems. These never changed.

Policymakers may have been slower to adopt Keynes' ideas on demand management, but his new theory was immediately taken up by economists all over the world, notably in the United States, which during and after World War II was practically the only place that mattered. However, his most influential followers did not simply drop all their existing ideas and adopt Keynes uncritically. They integrated parts of his theory into their own and used elements of the old "classical" theory to make sense of his thinking. The result was not just a new version of Keynesian theory, but an approach to analyzing the economy that evolved continually from 1940 through to the 21st century. Keynesianism meant different things to different economists. His ideas were important because they were not only essential for policy, but they also opened up a new way of analyzing economic activity that could be developed in many ways, both by economists who agreed with the conclusions he reached and by ones who did not.

While, as mentioned earlier, some economists see this as the creation of a bastard Keynesianism, it is also possible to perceive this as an inevitable and normal process. Moreover, not only is this natural, it is probably also something of which Keynes would have approved, even if he might have quarreled with details. He encouraged others to develop his work, even economists who were adapting his ideas in different ways. His was a creative mind that did not keep still. As early as 1937, he told Joan Robinson that he was getting himself into an outside position in relation to his book and that his ideas were already moving on. This was consistent with the view of his Bloomsbury friends that a subject was never considered closed. Had he lived longer, he would likely have developed new ideas in response to new challenges that arose, which suggests that the notion of "bastard" Keynesianism is misconceived. It is possible that the insights found in the *General Theory* can legitimately be developed in different ways.

The tragedy of Keynes' early death in 1946, little more than a month before his 63rd birthday, is not that he was unable to defend the *General Theory* against critics; it is that we have been deprived of the new creative insights and ideas that he might have developed later in life. Given his creativity, it is foolish to speculate on what these might have been.

AGGREGATE DEMAND

If Keynesianism evolves as generations of economists apply it to new problems, what can we still learn from Keynes?

As we have seen, when challenged after the *General Theory* was published, Keynes argued that the main feature of his theory was that it dealt with a world in which we know very little about the future. In short, he argued that saving and investment—decisions about the accumulation of wealth—cannot be based on rational calculation, because the information needed for such decisions is not available. As a result, and contrary to the claims of those who believed markets could solve all economic problems, there could be no presumption that entrepreneurs' decisions about investment would be consistent with savers' decisions about how much they wished to save.

Even if we accept this argument because we know that the future is not predictable, there remains the question of how we respond. Keynes had his own solution: to construct a theory on what would now be called "behavioral" micro-foundations, drawing on his own observations of how people behaved when faced with uncertainty that made rational calculation impossible. However, other economists —some calling themselves Keynesians, others not doing so —developed different ideas to tackle the same problem, modifying his theories in ways they thought either made them more rigorous or more consistent with data. For example, many economists believed that models based on calculations of probability could provide valuable insights into decision-making, even if they were not ideal. Others saw this as a betrayal of Keynes' key insight, arguing that it was necessary to stay much closer to Keynes' own approach to the problem. Their critics labeled this position "fundamentalist"—terminology comparing different interpretations of the *General Theory* with differences in the interpretation of religious texts.

A useful example here is the Nobel Prize winner and former Chief Economist at the World Bank, Joseph Stiglitz. He was trained at MIT, the home of Samuelson, Solow, and Modigliani, placing him at the center of the American Keynesian establishment. Together with several co-authors, Stiglitz used mathematical models in which uncertainty was analyzed in terms of probability distributions. He showed that if people have different amounts of information, markets cannot work in the manner assumed by the people Keynes described as "classical" economists: the free-market allocation of resources will generally not be efficient. Such theories support government interventions that are in line with those Keynes supported, but should we regard Stiglitz as a Keynesian? From a "fundamentalist" perspective, his use of probability models goes against Keynes' belief that behavior under uncertainty cannot be reduced to calculations of probabilities. On the other hand, it can be argued that, although Stiglitz used mathematical techniques that were not known in Keynes' day, he produced conclusions supporting Keynes' insights about the way the economic system works or does not work. So what should we conclude? The case can be argued either way.

The key feature of Keynesianism is arguably the notion that there can be too little aggregate demand to support full employment. In the *General Theory,* he associated himself with a sidelined, unorthodox tradition, running from the philosopher Bernard Mandeville in the early 18th century and Robert Malthus, famous for his principle of population at the beginning of the 19th century, to his contemporary, J. A. Hobson, best known for his theory of imperialism, which inspired Bolshevik leader, Vladimir Ilyich Lenin. Keynes described these under-consumptionists, so-called because they believed that consumption could be too low and saving too high, as a "brave army of heretics" who had "preferred to see the truth obscurely and imperfectly rather than to maintain error."*

However, perhaps a more telling example of traditional attitudes is John Stuart Mill, who was so influential that he came close to defining what orthodoxy was in Victorian Britain. Mill argued that people could be in a position to

---

* GT, 371.

spend money but might choose not to because they were apprehensive about what would happen in the near future. This might be because—anticipating the course of the business cycle—they expected prices to fall and, as a result, they could gain from postponing their spending: because, if they waited before spending their money, they would later be able to buy more goods for the same amount of money. Mill explained this idea very clearly, but elsewhere in his work, he held to the orthodox view that saving would normally get channeled into the pockets of those who wanted to invest. If we take Mill as our standard of comparison (and in this respect Keynes' teacher, Marshall, followed Mill pretty closely), then Keynes claimed that a phenomenon previously believed to be temporary was potentially long-lasting and sufficiently important that it was necessary to develop a more elaborate theory and to make it much more central to economics. The determination of the level of aggregate demand was not a problem that could be ignored because periodic shortages of aggregate demand were a fundamental feature of a capitalist economy. Economics needs a theory of aggregate demand because rational calculation is not always possible.

If this is the essence of Keynesianism, then much of what fits under this label can be seen as a legitimate interpretation of Keynes' ideas. The Americans who integrated his theory of the multiplier into theories of long-run stagnation in the 1930s and 1940s were taking his claim seriously that a theory of aggregate demand was needed. So too were those who struggled to create Keynesian theories based on models of individuals optimizing behavior in the second half of the 20th century, even though they were doing so in different ways and not always making precisely the same assumptions that Keynes himself made. It is therefore entirely reasonable to view Stiglitz's analyses of asymmetric information as being in the spirit of Keynes, and for Summers to look back, not to Keynes himself, but rather to Hansen and arguments about long-term stagnation in the 1940s. This is what it means for Keynesianism to be evolving.

TAKING RESPONSIBILITY

Diagnosis of the problems facing capitalist economies requires technical arguments about how the economy works. However, if we are to go further and argue for measures to solve these problems, technical arguments about how the economy works need to be set alongside the moral arguments. Running through all of Keynes' work, from *Economic Consequences of the Peace* to his final writing on policy, is the claim that governments need to take responsibility for things that otherwise will not get done. Keynes' diagnosis of how the capitalist system worked was that co-ordination of saving and investment was the main thing that would not be done if the state did not step in; therefore, the state had a responsibility to maintain the level of aggregate demand to ensure that resources, including labor, were fully utilized.

Claiming that the government should take action to manage the level of aggregate demand raises the further question of capitalism versus socialism. Today, people often associate socialism with the Soviet-style of communism, seeing the alternative as free-market capitalism. Faced with such a choice, it is easy to construct a moral case for capitalism. This system stands for freedom, while communism represents a denial of freedom. If this is combined with the argument that capitalism is more efficient in producing the goods and services people need, the case for capitalism as a preferable option seems clear-cut.

Here, Keynes proved a useful guide. At one point in the 1920s, he planned to write a book on capitalism. Unfortunately, he never found time, presumably because he was too busy with more urgent tasks, and all we have are rough notes he left behind. However, scattered across many newspaper and journal articles, he wrote a lot about capitalism in relation to socialism, which gives a clear picture of his position. His views are still relevant today because they provide a much more nuanced view of capitalism that resonates with many of our modern concerns.

The starting point in understanding Keynes' view of capitalism is that he saw it as an evolving system comprising a complex set of institutions. They include not only markets but also corporations (themselves governed by evolving sets of rules), households, government, the legal system, and more. Take away some of these institutions, and capitalism as we know it would not function. Even markets are complex organizations. In other words, capitalist economies involve much more than simply the absence of government regulation. This is well illustrated by what happened when the institutions of Soviet society collapsed in the early 1990s. The result was not the sudden emergence of free, competitive markets but chaos, unemployment, a fall in living standards, and a dramatic reduction in life expectancy. Socialism fell without putting the institutions necessary for a successful capitalist economy in its place. Eventually, those institutions were established, but the ones that emerged in the new Russia were not identical to those in other capitalist economies.

One implication of this is that we should see government activity and institutional reform not as an interference with a pristine "free-market" economy, but as part of the normal evolution of a capitalist economy. Reforms and interventions may be successful or unsuccessful, but there is no reason they should be considered inconsistent with capitalism. This means there is no basis for the argument that management of aggregate demand is necessarily incompatible with a free-market economy. On the contrary, Keynes believed such policies were essential if capitalism were to survive. Given the obvious attraction to many people of the virtues of sharing and ensuring that no one lacked the resources for a good life, both associated with socialism, Keynes argued that capitalism needed to perform better than socialism if it were to gain popular support.

As was explained when discussing the *General Theory*, Keynes believed that capitalism was important as a guarantor of freedom. This was a value he cherished and never abandoned. However, this does not mean that he found capitalism attractive. He did not. Even though he was very good at money-making, Keynes considered the pursuit of money for its own sake distasteful. In a BBC radio broadcast after the great crash of 1929, he said, "The spectacle of capitalists, striving to become liquid as it is politely called, that is to say pushing their friends and colleagues into the chilly stream, to be pushed in their turn by some yet more cautious fellow from behind, is not an edifying sight."* Capitalism was also suspect because setting a price on

* The Collected Writings of John Maynard Keynes, vol. XXI, 90.

everything was to devalue some of the more important things in life. Thus Keynes denounced the effects of capitalism on art in strong terms: "The exploitation and incidental destruction of the divine gift of the public entertainer by prostituting it to the purposes of financial gain is one of the worser [sic] crimes of present-day capitalism."[*] He wrote that "The love of money as a possession . . . [is] . . . a somewhat disgusting morbidity, one of those semi-criminal, semi-pathological propensities which one hands over with a shudder to the specialists in mental disease."[†] Money-making was worthwhile because it provided the means to a better life, not because it was inherently virtuous.

And yet, as has been explained, he recognized the need for capitalism and many of the values and activities that went along with it. This cautious attitude to capitalism, seeing it as morally suspect but essential, will resonate with many people after the experience of the 2008 financial crisis, when ill-conceived gambles by financial institutions would have started another Great Depression had governments not intervened. It should also resonate after the COVID-19 pandemic, when effective government action proved essential to support people economically in the face of measures needed to control the spread of the virus and to reduce the loss of life. Given the way new institutions need to be developed to cope with new challenges, from financial crises and pandemics to climate change, Keynes' belief that capitalism is not simply a set of competitive markets, but a complex set of institutions, should also make good sense.

* The Collected Writings of John Maynard Keynes, vol. XXVIII, 344.
† EP, 329.

In short, we should see Keynes as important for today not only because of the technical arguments he constructed about how capitalist economies sometimes fail to produce good outcomes, but also because he represents a vision of capitalism that transcends the conventional gulf between capitalism and socialism.

SUGGESTED READING

The best source for Keynes' writing on economics is the 30-volume *The Collected Writings of John Maynard Keynes* (Cambridge University Press, 1971-1989). Within this, it might seem that the best place to start would be Volume VII, *The General Theory of Employment, Interest and Money.* However, for a non-economist, it would probably be better to start with some of Keynes' shorter, more political, and more polemical writings. *Economic Consequences of the Peace*(Volume II) is the book through which many of Keynes' contemporaries first encountered Keynes and provides a lively introduction to his way of thinking. After that, it might be best to turn to the shorter papers reprinted in *Essays in Persuasion* (Volume IX), many of which were directed at a wide, educated readership. This volume, an expanded version of a book Keynes himself edited, contains a wide range of his writing on economic problems, including his arguments about combating depression (which were not discussed in the *General Theory*) and his attitudes towards socialism, communism, and liberalism. It also contains the essay, "Economic possibilities for our grandchildren," which anticipates the vision of the future that he outlined in Chapter 24 of the *General Theory*.

A side of Keynes not discussed in this book is his extensive writing on biography, most of which is collected in *Essays in Biography* (Volume X). This is very suitable for anyone who wants to learn more about Keynes and his writing while avoiding too much technical economics. Milton Friedman had expressed his appreciation for *A Tract on Monetary Reform* (Volume IV), which, though containing technical monetary analysis, was originally written, as was so much of Keynes' writing, for a general readership. For the other volumes, consult the list of titles or the index (Volume XXX). Finally, I would draw attention to a collection, edited by Donald Moggridge, one of the key people responsible for the *Collected Writings*, with the self-explanatory title, *Keynes on the Wireless* (Palgrave Macmillan, 2010), which contains transcriptions of short talks aimed at the general public. These offer a very direct entry into Keynes' thinking.

Turning to the secondary literature, the starting point has to be the biographies by Robert Skidelsky and Donald Moggridge. Skidelsky's is in three volumes: *John Maynard Keynes: Hopes Betrayed, 1883-1929*; *John Maynard Keynes: The Economist as Saviour, 1920-1937*; *John Maynard Keynes: Fighting for Freedom, 1937-1946* (or *Fighting for Britain, 1937-1946* in the British edition) (Macmillan, 1983, 1992, 2000). This was followed by an abridged single-volume edition, *John Maynard Keynes, 1883-1946: Economist, Philosopher, Statesman* (Macmillan, 2003). Moggridge's is *Maynard Keynes: An Economist's Biography* (Routledge, 1992). Both biographies are outstanding and authoritative. The official biography by Roy Harrod, *The Life of John Maynard Keynes*

(Macmillan, 1951), published only five years after Keynes' death, is still worth reading, though readers might wish to note the assessment of the book's limitations made by Skidelsky in the Introduction to his first volume. Skidelsky also wrote a much shorter account of *Keynes* (Oxford University Press, Past Masters, 1996), and Moggridge did the same in *Keynes* (Fontana Modern Masters, 1976).

The global financial crisis produced a flurry of books on Keynes. Skidelsky's *Keynes: The Return of the Master* (Allen Lane, 2009) explains Keynes' relevance after the crisis. Peter Clarke's *Keynes: The Twentieth Century's Most Influential Economist* (Bloomsbury 2009) is an account by an eminent British historian. Although it cannot compete with the full biographies by Skidelsky and Moggridge, it is probably one of the best concise treatments of Keynes. Richard Davenport-Hines' *Universal Man: The Seven Lives of John Maynard Keynes* (William Collins, 2015) is an entertaining account that complements the one I have offered here, for it focuses on Keynes' life, playing down his role as an economist. And, for obvious reasons, including acknowledging a source on which many points in this book are based, I recommend Roger Backhouse and Bradley Bateman's *Capitalist Revolutionary: John Maynard Keynes* (Harvard University Press, 2011).

Though more of an academic treatment of Keynes than some works mentioned so far, *The Cambridge Companion to Keynes*, edited by Backhouse and Bateman (Cambridge University Press, 2006), is useful, as the essays it contains approach Keynes from many angles. Many of the chapters are on Keynes himself, but there are also discussions that relate to the history of Keynesian economics, something that few of the books discussed earlier do. Each has a useful bibliography. Anyone interested in Keynes' views on population should consult John Toye Keynes on population (Oxford University Press, 2000).

There is a large academic literature on the history of macroeconomics—the field that developed after World War II, centered on Keynesian economics—but much of this literature, including some things I have written, is technical and would quickly lose most non-specialists. Because they contain non-technical summaries of material that is usually treated more formally, I suggest the relevant chapters of two of my books, *The Ordinary Business of Life* (Princeton University Press, 2002), published outside North America as *The Penguin History of Economics* (Penguin, 2002); and *The Puzzle of Modern Economics* (Cambridge University Press, 2002). My account, in Chapter 4, of the emergence of American Keynesianism draws on material from my recent book, *Founder of Modern Economics: Paul A. Samuelson*, Volume I: *Becoming Samuelson, 1915-1948* (Oxford, 2017).

Although this contains much else, Michael Bernstein's *A Perilous Progress: Economists and Public Purpose in Twentieth Century America* (Princeton University Press, 2001) is useful for policymaking in the Keynesian era. For an account by a conservative participant (Chair of the Council of Economic Advisers under Presidents Nixon and Ford), see Herbert Stein's *The Fiscal Revolution in America* (University of Chicago Press, 1969). Angus Burgin's *The Great Persuasion: Reinventing Free Markets since the Depression* (Harvard University Press, 2012) covers the organized opposition to Keynesian ideas, involving Hayek and Friedman.

ABOUT THE AUTHOR

Roger Backhouse is Professor of the History and Philosophy of Economics at the University of Birmingham in the U.K. and Erasmus University Rotterdam in the Netherlands. He has published extensively on the history of modern economics, including *The History of Economics: A Course for Students and Teachers* (2017), *Capitalist Revolutionary: John Maynard Keynes* (2011), and *The History of the Social Sciences since 1945* (2010). He is a Fellow of the British Academy and has held a Research Fellowship at the London School of Economics.

A WORD FROM THE PUBLISHER

Thank you for reading *Simply Keynes!*

We hope this book offered an illuminating look into the life, ideas, and lasting influence of John Maynard Keynes, the visionary economist whose insights reshaped how we understand markets, money, and government.

If *Simply Keynes* deepened your appreciation for his brilliance or sparked your curiosity about the world of economic thought, we'd be delighted if you shared your reflections. Your review, whether on Amazon, Barnes & Noble, Kobo, Apple Books, Goodreads, or wherever you discover your books, helps other readers find *Simply Keynes* and engage with his remarkable legacy.

Thank you for supporting *Simply Charly's Great Lives* series, where we bring history's most influential thinkers and creators to life in ways that inspire new understanding.

Made in the USA
Monee, IL
04 November 2026

67378088R00085